THE
ISO
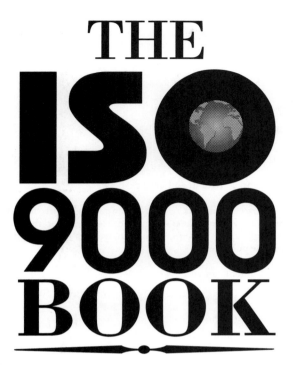
9000
BOOK

A GLOBAL COMPETITOR'S GUIDE TO COMPLIANCE & CERTIFICATION

JOHN T. RABBITT
PETER A. BERGH

QUALITY RESOURCES
A Division of The Kraus Organization Limited
White Plains, New York

Most Quality Resources books are available at quantity discounts when purchased in bulk. For more information contact:

Special Sales Department
Quality Resources
A Division of The Kraus Organization Limited
One Water Street
White Plains, NY 10601

800-247-8519   914-761-9600

Printed in the United States of America

97 96 95 94 93   10 9 8 7 6 5 4 3

Quality Resources   This book is also distributed by:
A Division of The Kraus Organization Limited
One Water Street   AMACOM Books, a division of
White Plains, NY 10601   American Management Association
914-761-9600   135 West 50th Street
800-247-8519   New York, NY 10020

∞

The paper used in this publication meets the minimum requirements of the American National Standard for Information Sciences — Permanence of Paper for Printed Library Materials, ANSI Z39.48-1984.

ISBN 0-8144-5175-6 (AMACOM Books)
ISBN 0-527-91721-4 (Quality Resources)

Library of Congress Cataloging–in–Publication Data

Rabbitt, John T.
    The ISO 9000 book : a global competitor's guide to compliance and
certification / John T. Rabbitt & Peter A. Bergh.
       p.   cm.
    Includes index.
    ISBN 0-527-91721-4 (Quality Resources : acid-free). — ISBN 0-8144-5175-6
(AMACOM : acid-free)
    1. Quality control — Standards. 2. Manufactures — Quality control — Standards.
3. Total quality management.   I. Bergh, Peter A. II. Title
TS156.R25 1993   93-14904
658.5'62 — dc20   CIP

Dedication

*To the employees of The Foxboro Company whose
dedication to creating a World Class Enterprise
enabled this story to be told.*

*And, to Charlotte, Deborah, and our families for
their tremendous patience and encouragement
throughout the duration of this project.*

Contents

4 • The Road To Discovery 45

5 • How Will We Ever Be Ready In Time? 77

6 • What Do They Really Mean? 119

Appendix 1 – Are You Ready? 135

Appendix 2 – For More Information 158

Index 159

Preface

The "good old days" are gone. Your customers are changing in response to new global competitive pressures. Some of your customers might already have asked you about the ISO 9000 series quality standards and your intentions in this regard. You are not alone. No matter what business you are in, you will eventually be asked, "Are you ISO certified?" In the U. K., just about every business, from the large multinationals to the local rubbish collector, has pursued or is pursuing certification. These companies recognize that the certification mark will mean more business or, at minimum, survival. It is estimated by an ISO 9000 certification agency that, in the U. S. alone, about 500,000 operations will need to achieve certification in the near future. This does not include the smaller operations that will eventually seek certification.

Possibly, your experience with today's competitive reality has led you to pick up this book. The more you read about ISO 9000, the more you begin to realize that it is not rocket science. The standard's vagueness, however, can be unnerving as you search for specifics. The reality is that only *you* can interpret the requirements as they relate to your business. It is a common misunderstanding that ISO 9000 is about doing what you say you do and documenting it period. This is only partially correct. You need to ensure that you really *do* what you claim you do, all the time, and that you have addressed some specific requirements as well. There is no single method for meeting ISO 9000 requirements; nor is there a single manual you can buy that will ensure certification. You are the only one who can bring your organization into compliance, and it is our hope that this book will help you get there with a minimum of pain.

Our intention is to provide you with a working understanding of ISO 9000, its requirements, and methodologies for compliance. We have drawn upon our team experiences at The Foxboro Company, one of the first major U.S. manufacturers to achieve ISO 9001 certification. We have also included types of questions that you might encounter when the auditors do come to visit you.

This book is not just about ISO 9000 certification: it is also about creating a sound business, one that will satisfy your customers. ISO 9000 is one of the tools you can use in your TQM journey. The certificate is a "seal of approval" that makes your customers feel better when they do business with you. Ultimately, this book is about improving your bottom line. Whether you are a Fortune 500 manufacturer, a local car dealership, or grocery store, we believe that ISO 9000 will affect you. The choice to pursue certification is yours. We hope this book will help you assess the relevance of the standard to your operation and help you achieve certification should you decide to pursue it.

1

How Did We Get Here?

ISO 9000 is more than just a standard. It reflects a well-organized operation with trained and motivated people. It is the new challenge. Those who move quickly will enjoy the fruits that result from being a leader. Those who defer will feel the pain of lost business. But beyond that, it's about running your business guided by common-sense principles that have existed for most of this century.

To put ISO 9000 in its proper perspective, it is useful to examine the evolution of manufacturing. The following is a nonacademic perspective.

From Farm to Factory

The first "manufactured" products were relatively simple, and a single craftsman would assemble and test the complete product. Usually, the craftsman was the only supplier in town for his specific product. His customers knew where he lived, he made house calls, and the entire village knew his family history. Times were great if you didn't mind ill-fitting, expensive, and hard-to-get material goods. It was just a matter of time before someone would realize that if all the craftsmen were moved into a single location, more could be produced at reduced costs.

A short time later, Samuel Slater arrived from England and started the first U.S. textile mill in Rhode Island. Since then nothing has been the same. Slater learned the secret of building machines for specific tasks and the use of low-cost farm labor to run them. Soon, all over New England's fast moving streams, those tiny mills became brick textile monoliths producing good, inexpensive textile goods.

Just as mass production was being born, Fred Taylor discovered that breaking tasks down into smaller elements, providing specific tools, and linking them closely would result in increased production. The United States was in a very rapid growth stage and experienced unprecedented demand for its cheap goods. Wave after wave of mostly non-English speaking and untrained immigrants flowed into the work force. Industry at that time was new and its leaders saw no alternative to Taylorism. The new industries as well as the nation grew from this base of low-cost, low-skilled labor.

As organizations grew, planning was split off from the production function it was meant to serve. Walls were erected to reduce the noise for the accountants and planners. Later those walls turned into offices with doors. New products were being designed in locations away from the production process, which made communications more difficult. With an overwhelming demand for goods, sins of waste and poor quality were quickly forgiven as new and less expensive products rolled out to meet an insatiable demand.

Enlightened Manufacturing

Much earlier in this century, the visionary, Henry Ford, saw a different way of conducting business. He expounded on the ideas of continuous improvement and waste reduction. In his book, *Today and Tomorrow*, written in 1926, he discusses how the concepts of process and linked flows were introduced and practiced. Ford drove his organization to continually look at the entire process and to continually work to improve each step. He knew his business and insisted that his employees do the same.

Ford felt that his employees and customers were one and the same, and unless an organization took care of its employees, it would destroy itself. He also believed that satisfying his customers was the greatest service he could provide, that satisfaction came from a continually lower cost of ownership, and that the world belonged to those who provided this service.

In 1908, the first Model T was introduced at a material cost of $850 and by 1924 he had not only dramatically improved the reliability of the vehicle, but had driven the material costs down to $290. Ford finished production of the Model T in 1927 and had sold more than 15,000,000 units.

Ford also pioneered the concepts of Process Integrity, Total Quality Control, Just In Time (JIT) and Kanban feed systems. He never allowed more than one shift's worth of material on the assembly floor. "Our production cycle is about eighty-one hours from the mine to the finished machine in the freight car." Today, that is about how long it takes to move the average material through incoming inspection. Ford also established the concepts of waste of inventory, energy conservation, employee training, employee safety, and cleanliness on the job site.

When asked to give advice to someone starting out (and the reason for his success), Ford said, "If we do that which is before us to do in the best way that we know, that is, if we faithfully try to serve, we do not have to worry about anything else. The future has a way of taking care of itself."

The Boom Years

After Ford created his eighth wonder of the world, bankers and stockbrokers began the process of speculation and uncontrolled borrowing. Meanwhile, the public adopted the Roaring '20s mind-set of "live for today." This nonproductive activity eventually caused the collapse of the capital market and drove the country into the depression of the 1930s.

For the next 10 years people lived conservatively. As World War II created a new demand for goods as well as shortages, the U.S. economy began to recover. The government created war-related jobs and rationed consumer goods to keep inflation down while participating in the destruction of a large segment of the world's industrial capacity. By the end of World War II, the U.S. had enjoyed four years of full employment. However, the little opportunity for consumer spending created an enormous capital base and a high demand for consumer goods. In addition, the troops came home and started buying goods from our intact U.S. factories at an unprecedented rate. The U.S. government then lent money to selected, war-ravaged countries to buy goods from the only remaining intact industry base, which was the U.S.

This resulted in an unparalleled shortage of goods. New inexperienced manufacturers emerged as a result of the shortages and product quality continued to decline. For example the Kaiser-Frazer auto company was founded when a liberty ship builder teamed up with Joseph Frazer, a very successful car salesman from Packard and General Motors. They really didn't know anything about building cars, but that didn't stop them. Although the car they developed did have some innovative features, they still had not overcome technical issues such as hard steering, gear whine, and wheel shimmy. However, when the car was introduced, it sold as if there was no tomorrow. Demand subsided in the early 1950s, marking the demise of Kaiser-Frazer. The motto of the 1950s and 1960s was "Make the Schedule." This worked quite nicely for the U.S. economy as it grew at an extraordinary rate. Then in the mid-1960s, German "bugs" started popping up everywhere, followed by a series of Japanese "beetles."

The Japanese Listened

Japan's industrial base was destroyed by the end of World War II. The country was occupied, and its consumers were broke and out of work. Japan had nowhere to go but up. It actually employed a recovery strategy that typifies most growing nations, and there are clear transition points. In the 1950s, Japan focused on low-cost, labor-intensive, low-technology industries like textiles. Meanwhile, U.S. quality gurus Deming and Juran were teaching lessons on process control and management throughout Japan.

During the 1960s, the Japanese had amassed enough capital to engage in a "Large Scale Manufacturing" based strategy that focused on productivity improvements. During the 1970s they developed flexible manufacturing strategies that incorporated both the "Scales" strategy with the

"Variety" approach. Meanwhile, cheap labor was becoming a thing of the past. Japanese industry was moving beyond Ford's concepts into new frontiers. Concurrently, the U.S. was becoming infatuated with computers and their promise of effortless salvation.

> **"Listen to me, and in five years you**
> **will be competing with the West.**
> **Keep listening, and soon the West will**
> **be demanding protection from you."**
>
> *W. Edwards Deming, speaking to 45 key*
> *Japanese industrialists at a seminar in 1950*

American industry believed the computer salvation story until the late 1980s. Ironically, during the early 1980s, the computer industry was already in the process of replacing massive computer-driven shop floor control systems with JIT and Kanban, but they weren't telling, lest they shoot the golden goose. In fact, a computer-industry pioneer was told not to make a speech at an industrial conference on JIT for fear of damaging the industry. The U.S. was losing the race, and it wasn't until the late 1970s that the lessons learned by the Japanese started beating the daylights out of our industries. The weak players were the first to feel the impact.

The Declining Years

In 1979, the Ford Motor Company recalled more cars than it produced. In consumers' eyes, "Ford" became an acronym for "Fix or Repair Daily" and Ford's customers were getting a "Better Idea" from the competition. The effect on the business was devastating as thousands were laid off, and industry observers were wondering if they were witnessing the demise of the Founding Father of the automotive industry. Meanwhile, our consumer electronics industry was rapidly migrating offshore. According to U.S. Labor Department statistics, during the mid-1980s, many new jobs were created, giving the illusion that the economy was on an even keel. But these were low-wage service sector jobs, and the U.S. was losing 20,000 to 30,000 manufacturing jobs a month to foreign manufacturing.

In 1980, Ford executives asked Dr. Deming to come in and breathe some life into their failing entity. Dr. Deming gave them some very sound advice that began with knowing their process and gaining stability within their operation. By the mid-1980s, the Japanese were evolving their "Variety and Speed" strategy. General Motors (GM) had determined that they would automate out of existence the very thing that Ford had considered his most valuable asset — people. GM made a big bet on strategies such as MAP (manufacturing automation protocol) as the answer to this latest competitive challenge, even though there was clear evidence that the organizations that were beating them in the marketplace were employing a different approach.

> **"You can always count on the Americans to do the right thing! ...but, only after they have tried everything else..."**
>
> *Winston Churchill*

By 1985, Ford had achieved a remarkable rebound and had just out-earned GM. By 1987, Ford boosted profits by an additional 40%. What caused this remarkable turnaround? Ford gained control of its processes and met a minimum set of *customer expectations*, which is the essence of ISO 9000.

It's About More Than Just ISO 9000

Currently, the Europeans are banding together to create the world's largest market with new barriers. The Asian basin is afire with development and growth. Awareness and recognition are growing for the need to rethink how we run our businesses — to refocus on elimination of nonvalue-adding functions and to put the customer above all else. The emergence and growing global acceptance of ISO 9000 conveniently provides a framework for businesses to assess where they are and where they want to be. In addition, conformance to the standard demonstrates a minimum level of acceptable performance that is universally recognized and accepted. The following chapters will describe how the pursuit of ISO 9000 is simply good business practice.

2

Why All The Fuss?

The ISO 9000 standards represent the common denominator of business quality that is accepted internationally. In 1987 they were adopted by the International Organization for Standardization (ISO). ISO 9000 certification demonstrates the capability of a supplier to control the processes that determine the acceptability of the product or service being supplied.

By mid-1992, more than 30,000 European companies had been certified and the numbers are growing dramatically. In contrast, there are only about 300 U.S. facilities that have achieved certification. While certification to the standard is not mandatory in the EC, one can expect that when a certified supplier is competing with a noncertified supplier, the certified one will be preferred.

The Basics

ISO 9000 is a foundation for running a business well. Just as different types of structures require different foundations, so do different businesses. Thus, the ISO 9000 standard is presented in five documents: ISO 9000 through ISO 9004. The standards ISO 9001 through ISO 9003 apply to enterprises according to the scope of their activities. ISO 9004 and the ISO 9000-X family are documents that provide specific guidelines for specific industrial applications, as seen in Figure 2.1.

Of the three ISO 9000 standards, ISO 9001 is the most comprehensive in scope, confirming process conformance from the initial development of a product through production, test, installation, and servicing.

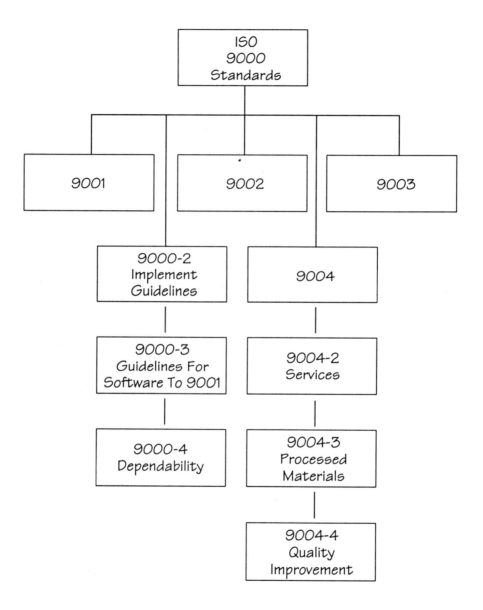

Figure 2.1 The ISO 9000 family of standards.

ISO 9002 covers only the procurement, production, and installation portion of your business. Both standards require the same degree of conformance to their respective scope of activity. For example, when comparing two suppliers of a commodity item, such as paper, if one has ISO 9001 certification and the other has ISO 9002 certification, it does not mean that the ISO 9001 operation has a better process. However, if you require the producer to provide design work for you or you require extensive service support, then the ISO 9001 certified supplier is the supplier of choice, as ISO 9002 does not provide for a review of these areas.

ISO 9003, unlike the previous two, addresses only the production process and has a significantly lower conformance requirement. This standard is somewhat controversial and many feel that it generally undermines the entire standard — insofar as a major certification agency in this country will no longer certify to this standard. We would be very suspect of a supplier who could only reach ISO 9003 and could not bring its procurement activities under control. Figure 2.2 shows the relationships among the three standards.

As you work your way through the standard, you may find yourself asking, "What do they really mean?" The truth is that it is intentionally vague in certain ways, so it can accommodate just about any business operation. Recognizing this, the standard is devised so that you can meet its basic requirements by operating your business your way. ISO 9000 defines basic principles for a sound business operation and you must interpret it according to your business. You are the expert, and only you can define how you operate. ISO 9000 requires that you simply operate in the manner that you say you do while meeting certain basic requirements. This is not rocket science by any stretch.

There is a great deal of misinformation about the standard in the business community. At the time of this writing, approximately 300 sites in the U.S. are certified, yet more than 5,000 consultants claim ISO 9000 expertise — this just doesn't make sense. On the other hand, although you can't buy certification through a consultant, the best ones can be very helpful in advising you and seeing you through the process.

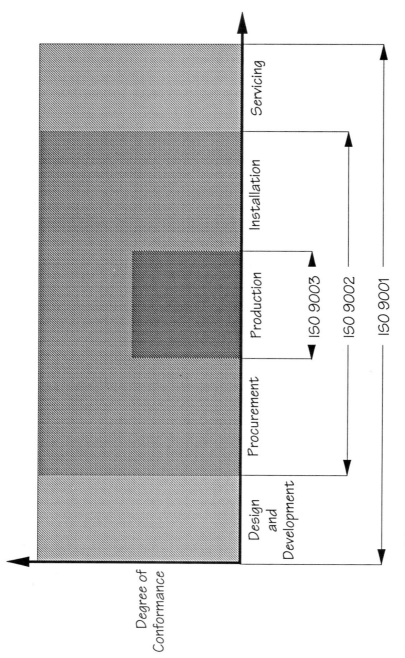

Figure 2.2 Scope of the ISO 9000 standards.
Source: Det Norske Veritas.

The 20 Elements

The ISO 9000 standard focuses on 20 aspects of a quality program that are subject to a rigorous audit during the certification process. Each section relates to a specific aspect of satisfying customers. When trying to determine how each section applies to your organization, ask yourself how it relates to your customer's expectations. The following 20 elements are contained in Section 4 of the ISO 9000 standard document.

4.1 • Management responsibility
4.2 • Quality system
4.3 • Contract review
4.4 • Design control
4.5 • Document control
4.6 • Purchasing
4.7 • Purchaser supplied product
4.8 • Product identification and traceability
4.9 • Process control
4.10 • Inspection and testing
4.11 • Inspection, measuring, and test equipment
4.12 • Inspection and test status
4.13 • Control of nonconforming product
4.14 • Corrective action
4.15 • Handling, storage, packaging, and delivery
4.16 • Quality records
4.17 • Internal quality audits
4.18 • Training
4.19 • Servicing
4.20 • Statistical techniques

The Customer's Perspective

The following is a brief explanation of each element of the standard from a customer's perspective.

Figure 2.3 ISO 9000 prevents this.

4.1 • *Management responsibility* – Who is responsible for ensuring that the product or service is what I ordered and when? Who ensures that your system is effectively managed?

4.2 • *Quality system* – Is the quality system in place to ensure that everything delivered to me is as you said it would be? How do you make sure?

4.3 • *Contract review* – What is your system for ensuring that what marketing and sales sold me is actually what I will be getting and when?

4.4 • *Design control* – Show me how you designed the product and how you ensure it does what you say it does. Is there agreement between the designers and salespeople that it works as they claim? If you make changes to the design, how is it determined that my product is still acceptable?

4.5 • *Document control* – How do you inform manufacturing of the requirements and materials for building the product? If you make a change to the requirements, how is that communicated? If I need parts, will you be able to tell me what to order? If changes are made in the material requirements, how is manufacturing informed of how to test it or when to acquire the new parts? Will the service organization know which parts are needed for a repair job?

4.6 • *Purchasing* – Can you show me how you are making sure that your purchasing group is buying what your designers and engineers are specifying? How do you know you are buying from a supplier who makes good product and delivers it on time?

4.7 • *Purchasing of supplied product* – Show me how you protect, store, and maintain you materials. If there is a problem with the materials, show us how you fix it.

4.8 • *Product identification and traceability* – Show me how you ensure my materials don't get mixed up with others and that they are really what you ordered. How do you check that they are what the drawings say they are? How do you ensure the correct materials are used when building my product?

4.9 • *Process control* – Show me that you have procedures in place to build my product properly — I'm especially concerned with procedures on critical items relative to the manufacture of my product. Do you know how to make my product correctly and can you distinguish between the right way and the wrong way? Do you know when you are making junk? Do you have any points in the process where you cannot tell by inspection that the product is acceptable? How do you handle this? They should be written down so people can easily access them if they have any questions or if they want to train someone.

4.10 • *Inspection and testing* – How do you ensure that I will receive what I ordered? Have you verified that my product will work as promised? I mean really tested — can you show me?

4.11 • *Inspection, measuring and test equipment* – How do you ensure that the equipment you are using to test the correctness of my product is accurate? How are you doing this?

4.12 • *Inspection and test status* – Show me how it is indicated on my product that it was tested.

4.13 • *Control of nonconforming product* – When it is discovered that part of my product doesn't work or fit as it should, is there an established procedure for fixing it? Does everyone know what to do when it is fixed? I would like it to be retested. How do you know it didn't get mixed in with other products after you discovered it wasn't correct?

4.14 • *Corrective action* – If you find a problem with a product, what is the procedure for ensuring it doesn't happen again? Are you writing new procedures and training people to ensure it doesn't occur again?

4.15 • *Handling, storage, packaging, and delivery* – How are you ensuring my product was built properly and that it is packaged and stored to prevent damage? Can you make sure the delivery process keeps my product from being damaged?

4.16 • *Quality records* – Do you have procedures to document the quality of my product? This should include the raw materials records. Could I find these records quickly if that was our agreement?

4.17 • *Internal quality audits* – How do you ensure that you are running your operation as you claim? Have you trained a group of people to review your operation? Can you show me records that demonstrate that attention has been given to the critical areas? Can you show me where the management in the area has fixed a problem discovered by the audit team?

4.18 • *Training* – Prove to me that the people who built and tested my product are trained. Do they know all the critical aspects of my product and how it should work? Has the supervisor agreed that the person is trained properly?

4.19 • *Servicing* – If you told me you could service my product, how would you do that? Can you ensure that you will conduct your operations as well as you did when you first built my product (i.e., good parts, delivered on time, tested again)? Can you ensure that my product will be worked on only by someone who has been properly trained?

4.20 • *Statistical techniques* – If you are using statistical techniques to validate that my product is good, could you show me that they work? Does everyone who is using these techniques know what to do when it is indicated that the process is out of control or moving outside the control limits?

Hopefully, this brief look at ISO 9000 from a customer's perspective provides a working approach to the standard. To avoid confusion, just keep asking yourself, what does my customer want?

ISO 9000 — An Everyday Example

One example that demonstrates how ISO 9000 applies to an everyday situation is having the brakes of your car worked on at the local garage. You remember a local garage's ad for a special on brake repairs; in addition, you recall a neighbor speaking highly of the place.

As you approach the front counter of the shop, your journey through ISO 9000 begins. The clerk listens to your experience with the brakes as well as about your car. He informs you that your car will require metallic brake pads that will cost extra. You agree to go ahead with the job and the clerk promises your car will be ready in one hour.

As you wait, you mull over your main concerns: Will the car stop properly? Will the repair cost more than was stated? Will they complete the work in an hour? This is what ISO 9000 is all about — confidence that the task will be done *as promised.* The ISO 9000 standard encompasses many details that would easily be taken for granted. As illustrated in the rest of this example, the standard requires that attention be paid to every aspect of the brake job

You realize that when you picked up the advertisement, there was a management structure that made sure the business ran well and that quality methods and practices are used, which gave the garage a good reputation. You want to be confident that the mechanic knows where to get the work order papers for your car, and actually gets *your* car. Hopefully the mechanic has been trained to drive your car onto the ramp properly, disassemble the brakes, and inspect them to ensure nothing else is wrong. Then that the mechanic goes to the proper documents and determines which brake shoes are right for your car and retrieves the parts from a bin with the shoes correctly identified. You would expect that if a mechanic tried to use some parts that ended up not fitting, he would have removed them from stock rather than putting them back in and passing the problem on to you. You hope that this person can assemble the brakes to the proper torque requirements and finally test them by driving your car around the block. You expect to be provided with a check sheet of the items tested and that your car was parked in a safe place. This section with the mechanic covers many of the twenty ISO 9000 elements.

4.1 • *Management responsibility* – Someone is in control ensuring that the organization is selling products and services in the fashion it claims to.

4.2 • *Quality system* – The owners of the operation have a quality system in place to ensure their business operates as indicated. When you approached the counter, the clerk created a contract with you. This person was knowledgeable about the product and communicated with the shop to know approximately how long it would be. The clerk had the training and documents to know that your car required metallic pads, where you should leave your car, and what to do when you returned to pick it up. This person was also willing and able to address your further questions and concerns.

4.3 • *Contract review* – Ensures that the work performed by the mechanic was what you had agreed to with the clerk.

4.4 • *Design control* – Ensures that the brakes placed on your car were properly designed, tested, and documented so as to perform the job as specified.

4.5 • *Document control* – Ensures that the documents and reference books were available to the mechanic for the proper selection of materials and the appropriate testing.

4.6 • *Purchasing* – Ensures that the mechanic had the correct parts available.

4.8 • *Product identification and traceability* – Ensures that the brake linings retrieved from the stock bin were marked properly.

4.9 • *Process control* – There were established procedures for the mechanic to do the job, fill out the paperwork, find information on the materials, and access usable assembly instructions.

4.10 • *Inspection and testing* – The mechanic did some form of inspection and test to ensure that your new brakes were acting properly.

4.11 • *Inspection, measuring, and test equipment* – Ensures that the testing and measurement setting devices are calibrated to the correct torques and the right tools are being used to do it.

4.12 • *Inspection and test status* – Ensures that the check-off sheet is a working document and that tests were performed.

4.13 • *Control of nonconforming product* – Ensures that the mechanic knows what to do if a possible problem is detected with the material and how it should be treated and identified to prevent it from ending up on the other side of your car.

4.14 • *Corrective action* – Ensures that the mechanic and his management have a procedure for fixing known problems.

4.15 • *Handling, storage, packaging, and delivery* – The mechanic must know how to handle the brake pads before installation and ensure that they have been stored in a protected area. In addition, the mechanic must know where to put your car, keys and paperwork when completed.

4.16 • *Quality records* – The mechanic fills out a standard checklist, makes additional notes on the procedure being performed, and perhaps even has a place to record related issues for you to consider and for the shop to note.

4.17 • *Internal quality audits* – The supervisor should be regularly observing the areas to ensure that the mechanic has all the correct materials and documents and is performing tasks correctly.

4.18 • *Training* – This ensures that the mechanic had the proper training before working on your car and that the supervisor went over the task and verified that the mechanic was successful in all aspects of the job.

4.19 • *Servicing* – Ensures that the mechanic knows what to do if something doesn't work correctly with the new brakes.

4.20 • *Statistical techniques* – This ensures that metrics are kept regarding the quality of the service provided at the garage and are reviewed to ensure that the processes remain in control and that problem areas are quickly identified.

You notice an hour has passed. You go to the front desk. The clerk says, "Your car is coming out right now and we noticed that your driver's side windshield wiper was worn, so we replaced it free of charge, as our management believes your safety is paramount. Here are your keys and an itemized check sheet of all the tasks completed. This will also act as your warranty. Please note our toll-free number should you have any problems or wish to make an appointment for any of your other vehicles. Thank you for your patronage and please drive carefully."

**ISO 9000 alone didn't create
customer satisfaction,
but it was a foundation on which to build...**

That's what all the fuss is about!

This is a simple tale about brakes being fixed and a very happy customer in the end. It illustrated an ISO 9000 compliant organization taking care of the customer in a way that met the customer's expectations. However, it wasn't conformance to the ISO 9000 standard alone that made the customer pleased with having the brakes fixed. It was that extra touch of the 75¢ wiper being put on the car that showed that they cared. This was later reinforced when the clerk mentioned to drive carefully. By providing the customer with a special toll-free telephone number, the garage reinforced that it valued the business. These extra little items all exceeded his expectations, and the checklist reaffirmed the expectation of good value for the expected task. When you combine performance of the primary task to a normal expectation (ISO 9000 defined), and then go beyond that expectation, you end up with a very happy customer. That's what quality is all about — creating customer satisfaction.

ISO 9000, Quality, and the Baldrige

Although ISO 9000 certification can provide your customer with a degree of comfort and confidence about your process and your ability to deliver the product as promised, it also provides your organization with the ability to reduce costs, improve delivery, and increase speed. As stated earlier with the brakes example, ISO 9000 does not perform these modern day miracles by itself, but works within an overall quality model.

Renowned quality experts Deming, Juran, and Crosby have each promoted a set of 10-14 steps or points that they believe address the issue of quality. All these points or steps are valid and they share some common threads. We took the liberty of boiling them down to the seven critical ones listed below. Note that the first three positions are occupied by elements of ISO 9000.

The Seven Quality Success Factors

1. **Customer focus**
2. **Process versus results focus**
3. **Management commitment/responsibility**
4. **Continuous improvement**
5. **Less than 20% of problems caused by workers**
6. **Performance measures**
7. **Cross functional councils create constancy**

A company's position in the quality evolution is indicated by its level of employee involvement and market presence. ISO 9000 is at the very basic end of the quality evolution and provides you with stability and the minimum attributes for market survival, as shown in Figure 2.4. With ISO 9000 compliance and certification you will notice increased employee involvement and the ability to more easily correct problems, as we will describe in the following chapter.

ISO 9000 vs. The Baldrige

The following are some commonly asked questions related to ISO 9000 and the Malcolm Baldrige National Quality Award.

1 • Should we go for the Baldrige Award or ISO 9000 certification first?

Go for ISO 9000 compliance first. Achieving certification will help you prepare for the Baldrige. The 1992 applications for the Baldrige Award were down, and it was the feeling of the Baldrige committee that this was in response to companies going for ISO 9000 certification first.

2 • What's the difference between ISO 9000 and the Baldrige Award?

ISO focuses very closely on your internal processes, especially manufacturing, sales, administration, and technical support and services. The Baldrige places more emphasis on customer satisfaction and business results. The differences between the two are illustrated in Figure 2.5 and Figure 2.6.

3 • Do you have to be certified to ISO 9000 before going for the Baldrige?

The Baldrige assumes you have your processes under control and therefore awards relatively few points in this area. The Baldrige addresses the issues of customer satisfaction, business results, and the competitive aspects of gaining increased sales and profitability. ISO 9000 virtually ignores competitive positioning.

Figure 2.4 ISO 9000 is at the very basic end of the quality evolution, providing stability and the minimum attributes for market survival.

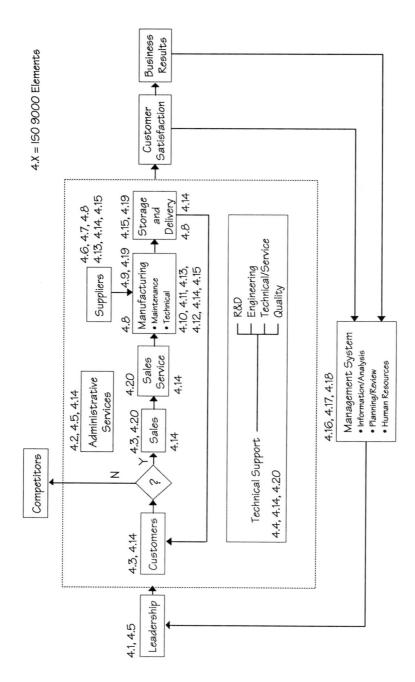

Figure 2.5 ISO 9000 vs. the Baldrige — ISO 9000 emphasis areas.
Source: Weyerhaeuser Company.

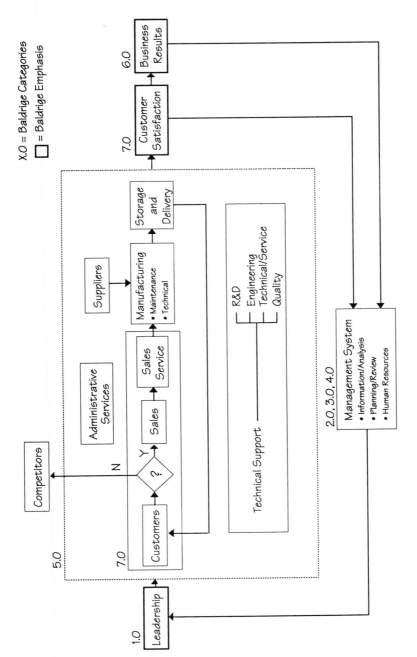

Figure 2.6 ISO 9000 vs. the Baldrige — Baldrige emphasis areas.
Source: Weyerhaeuser Company.

3

What If We Don't Do It?

What do the 320 million people of the European Community share?
What standard has every major industrialized nation adopted?
What is required to sell certain goods to the English government?
What could contribute to a significant boost to your bottom line?
What should you really comply with before winning the Baldrige?
What's being incorporated into U.S. Department of Defense and NATO purchasing requirements?
What is being incorporated into the Good Manufacturing Practices standards?

The answer: ISO 9000.

This chapter will review what ISO 9000 means to your operation and describes why you may be required to comply.

Good Business Sense, Even When Times Are Good

If your profits are up and business prospects look rosy, you may feel no motivation to change your operations. After all, pain is usually what motivates change. You may be leading your market thanks to new technology — but new technology is also soon-to-be-copied technology. It's unlikely that you'll enjoy those margins indefinitely. Success is great, but one of its main dangers is complacency. Now may be an ideal time to dive into the ISO 9000 compliance process. If your firm is experiencing falling sales or profits, then ISO 9000 may be an effective first step for turning the situation around.

The world has changed — in the 1950s and 1960s a business could operate based on the following formula.

$$\text{Product Cost} + \text{Desired Profit} = \text{Sales Price}$$

Within reason, you could name your price, and with the appropriate marketing support, you could derive your desired profit. Product cost was not a primary consideration in design or production, and niche marketing would support your sales price.

The 1990s present an entirely different business climate. Our once attractive formula for business success has been transposed.

$$\text{Sales Price} - \text{Product Cost} = \text{Profit}$$

Today, markets quickly set and drive prices down, and consumers have difficulty differentiating the performance and quality of competing products. Marketing efforts have mostly saturated consumers. Profit is now often a result of how well you can control and reduce your costs,

"No! I can't be bothered to see any crazy salesman.
We've got a battle to fight!"

Figure 3.1

which historically has been a weak link. Business in the 1990s will require you to employ every effort on *total cost reduction.* This means more than a purchase price variance on raw materials. It means reducing costs in administration, design, manufacturing—in every corner of your business. We previously listed some questions that address specific benefits of ISO 9000 certification. We will now examine three broad issues that encompass those specifics:

- European competitiveness.
- Market perception of your company's fitness.
- Internal organizational health.

European Competitiveness

Although it has been endorsed by the EC, ISO 9000 is not a European conspiracy to lock out foreign products. The ISO 9000 standard actually originated from the quality standards of the U.S. Department of Defense (MIL-Q9858) in the late 1950s. These standards were adopted by the British Standards Institution, and the scope was expanded to incorporate the entire business process and was designated as the British Standard 5750 code in 1979. The International Organization for Standardization adapted the British 5750 code and issued what is now called the ISO 9000 standard series in 1987.

Although ISO 9000 evolved technically in Europe, the International Organization for Standardization consists of members from more than 100 countries. At the time of this writing, an American from AT&T is chairing the group. This is a truly global standard.

What really makes Europe so pivotal in the development of the standard, and what in turn makes the standard so vital to businesses of all nations, is that the European Community has made the standard the standard law. An interesting chain of events has moved the standard into its present European prominence.

During the past 15 years, the European economies have lagged behind those of the U.S. and Japan. The Europeans recognized that trade barriers between their countries have undermined their ability to compete internationally and grow. Some European firms have as many as 12 distinct standards to comply with. Multiple standards discourage manufacturers from trading outside of their own, well-understood, smaller domestic markets, depriving them of the economies of scale that a large international market allows. By eliminating trade barriers, European manufacturers would have access to a $4 trillion market with more than 320 million potential customers. The bordering non-EC countries also recognized the benefits of a common market and the seven European Free Trade Association (EFTA) members petitioned to acquire a special trading arrangement with the EC. They have reached an agreement that means the new European market will consist of 19 countries (states of the EC) and a total of 380 million people. If the countries of the former Soviet block begin petitioning, we could easily witness the formation of a half-billion consumer market.

In June of 1985, the Europeans declared their intentions for barrier-free trade by December 31, 1992. No one expected that this would be anything but a complicated task requiring compromises among the EC member countries unlike any that had preceded them. Since the announcement, Europe has made significant progress, but many major hurdles remain, which probably won't be completely resolved until the turn of the century. One of these hurdles is the incorporation of a broad set of common standards into legislation. Upon acceptance, each piece of legislation becomes a "Legislated Directive" that can have an impact on any aspect of business within the EC. As the Legislated Directives are generated by the EC, they are then adopted by the member states and placed into national statutes. Only a handful of these directives were in place for 1993.

The European requirements for ISO 9000 product or industry compliance continues to evolve. For starters, the EC has specified classes of products that are either "regulated" or "nonregulated." Regulated products are those that have a health, safety, or environmental impact and are required to be manufactured under ISO 9000 conditions. Examples of regulated products are children's toys, computer terminals, and food packaging.

If you produce a nonregulated product, however, don't assume that ISO 9000 doesn't apply. ISO 9000 is quickly becoming the minimum requirement for doing business, regulated or not! In response to the varying technical standards for regulated products, the EC established the following groups to ensure harmonization among the standards: CEN for nonelectrical requirements (ISO 9000), CENELEC for electrical requirements, and ETSI for telecommunications standards. Figure 3.2 shows the relationship between these groups and the international standards bodies.

The EC has passed a series of general legislative directives and left the details up to groups like CEN to define. It is the purpose of these groups to harmonize the various standards such that all manufacturers could support a common requirement and thus allow free trade among the member states.

CEN adopted the ISO 9000 standards verbatim and renamed them as the EN 29000 series with its corresponding breakdown. CEN recognized that process stability and the robustness of the standard would deliver a better product, thereby, raising the general quality of European products throughout the community. One way to promote this standard was to encourage third-party certification.

> "The Commission has recognized the important role (quality assurance) techniques can play and so will not only promote their usage but will encourage the use of third party certification of quality systems when it is carried out in a transparent manner, inducing mutual recognition throughout the Community. Moreover, the commission considers that such techniques can also be used in legislation, either to enhance the credibility of a manufacturer's declaration or to complement, reduce or bring more flexibility to third party intervention in respect to the products themselves." (EOTC progress report of 1990)

To promote confidence in third-party certification, the EC established the EN 45000 series of standards to qualify testing labs and registrars. As a result, each member nation established a formal recommendation

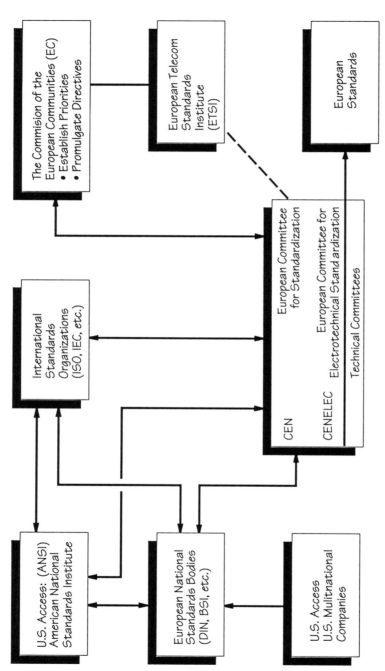

Figure 3.2 Relationship among standards bodies.

board that reports to the government. This board recommends various third-party certification agencies. Examples of these recommending boards are the Raad voor de Certificatie (RvC) of Holland, the National Accreditation Council for Certifying Bodies (NACCB) of the United Kingdom, and the Registrar Accreditation Board (RAB) of the U.S. Once a third-party agency is accepted by the board, it is listed as a *notified body* or *accredited registrar* in the EC product directives. The notified bodies or third-party certification agents can then provide a *recognized registration mark* of the sponsoring governmental agency. For example, the third-party registration firm of Det Norske Veritas (DNV) can provide a registration mark of the RvC (see Figure 3.3) or the NACCB to its customers who have undergone a successful ISO 9000 audit depending on the audit scheme used.

A careful look at all the directives indicates that process quality certification (ISO 9000) by a third party is generally not required. However, the blanket endorsement of the third-party certification process by the EC council and other EC legislative actions makes it a de facto requirement. For example, products sold within the EC will be subject to new legislation related to product liability and safety. The EC product liability directive states that a manufacturer, regardless of fault or negligence, is liable to a person who is harmed by a faulty product. The product safety directive requires manufacturers to monitor the safety of their products throughout the product's lifetime. The result of these two

Figure 3.3 Registration mark of the RvC issued by third-party registration firm Det Norske Veritas.

directives is that a manufacturer must document that it has maintained a defect-free manufacturing process. If a manufacturer is required to defend itself in a court and can demonstrate that through its processes and third-party certification that it did produce products in a defect-free environment and met the appropriate EC standards, it may be able to free itself of the liability and enjoy the appropriate liability protection afforded it under EC law. ISO 9000 requires that you've surveyed and carefully selected your suppliers as part of the *purchasing* requirement. For example, if a European manufacturer has four equivalent suppliers, three in Europe certified to ISO 9000 and one noncertified located in the U.S., do you think it would spend $5,000-$10,000 to send a review team to the U.S. just to maintain another supplier? More and more European purchase agreements will require demonstrated compliance to ISO 9000.

Market Perception of Your Company's Fitness

ISO 9000 certification will impact your domestic business in at least the following four areas:

1. Competition against suppliers who are certified.
2. Certified organizations focused on continuous improvement.
3. Media awareness.
4. Customer perception.

Competition Against Suppliers Who Are Certified

Usually, members of a sales force are trained to capitalize on the strengths of their products and organization. They are also made aware of the competitive issues affecting their organization. If you teach your sales people about ISO 9000 certification and explain why you are requiring certification from your suppliers for the parts that go into the products they sell, they will not hesitate to relate this to their customers. You will want to provide a copy of the certificate to each member of the sales team.

You may also want to coach them on how to discuss certification, such as with the following example.

In this example, you have two identical toasters, both certified by a reputable laboratory for safety. One toaster is manufactured in an ISO 9000 compliant environment, that is, the designs are correctly replicated to the manufacturing organization, the approved raw materials are purchased, the product is properly assembled by trained employees, tested properly, and packaged and transported according to procedures. The organization can make incremental improvements in the product because of its stable process. The customer has a high probability of receiving the product on time, with a low failure rate, and with an ideal mean-time-between-failure (MTBF).

If the same toaster is built in a noncertified facility, it cannot be demonstrated that its designs have been properly replicated by the manufacturing operations, that purchasing was done from a reliable supplier, or that it has been properly assembled by trained employees. There is nothing to show that it was tested properly or to current specifications. There were no guarantees that it was packaged or transported according to procedure. Given this environment, there is a higher probability of late deliveries, higher initial failure rates, and most likely a lower MTBF. One could easily conclude that the company is probably out of control, otherwise it would have been certified to ISO 9000.

Even though a supplier might have full approval for his product design, it does not necessarily mean the product is manufactured and tested to this design. The following are a couple of real-life examples.

Formerly, as the manufacturing manager for a company that was not yet compliant with a product safety standard (and law in some cities) called "LULU," I went to the sales organization for guidance to identify the first product to bring into compliance to minimize any potential losses. The head salesperson gave me some guidance but assured me that this new law would not affect the company's sales performance or his incentive plan. When I inquired how that was possible, he winked and opened his drawer. Out came an entire roll of LULU stickers he was placing on the products in his distribution center prior to shipment.

In another job as a new director of manufacturing, I decided to spend my second day on the assembly lines meeting the employees and going through the assembly process. This product spent most of its life in dark and damp locations and would accommodate 220 volts. It also carried a Canadian safety sticker. When I got to the end of the assembly line, I noticed that there was no earth-to-ground dielectric test being performed. This test ensures that customers are safe from shock. When I inquired why this test was not performed, I was told it was a pain to perform and it slowed things down, so my predecessor had removed it. I then asked how they were able to slip this by the visiting Canadian inspector, upon which I was told that when he showed up, they told him they weren't building anything for Canada then, and he went away.

If your buyers have a choice between buying from a certified or a noncertified supplier, and they choose the possibly cheaper, noncertified supplier's product, they may face a much grimmer liability situation.

Certified Organizations Focused On Continuous Improvement

In the 1990s, organizational success will be determined by a few key factors. One of these is speed. Execution speed includes the speed of product development, product upgrade and introduction, and even the more mundane functions such as responding to a customer inquiry. Speed will determine who are the profitable leaders and who are the less fortunate followers.

Speed comes from the repetition of well-defined tasks coupled with the continuous improvement of the supporting operating systems. If a competitor is able to perfect a working quality model before you do, they will begin to pick up competitive speed, and with speed comes distance. The longer you wait, the greater the distance you fall behind your competitors.

While their speed picks up, your organization, without the working model, will begin to slow down as you divert resources to brute-forcing results, all the while your resources become further diminished due to decreasing sales. Soon you are caught in a vicious cycle with the only

possible solutions being painful ones — if it's not too late altogether.

Here's an outline of such a decline. Your sales organization probably has a tough job winning business in a normal environment, where all competitors are on par. If your organization is having difficulties with product quality, response time, or delivery integrity, the first part of your salesperson's call time is usually spent apologizing and sorting the performance problems before being able to do his sales pitch on the benefits of your products. You are losing a lot of selling time and reducing the effectiveness of sales presentation time. And that's on top of the customer's displeasure with your late delivery, which violates the number one quality priority and for which this customer is now personally taking the heat from his management.

If the problem is persistent, your sales people may never get the chance to sell at all, or worse yet, not meet their sales incentive plan. You can burn through good sales people quickly and they will become excellent competitors who know all your weaknesses. It doesn't take long to lose a customer, but it takes quite a bit longer and requires more resources to get those customers back than if you had stabilized your business.

Media Awareness

Achieving ISO 9000 is a newsworthy event, especially when most firms don't make it on the first try — take full advantage of it. Consider the news of your certification just as you would any major event in your company, such as a major new product introduction or the appointment of a new senior executive. Get your marketing and communications specialists onboard early (plan on six months before certification), educate them, and let them educate the media in your industry and formulate the strategy to maximize the visibility of this landmark achievement. If you're thinking of the costs associated with advertising, think again. Save the money to fly your quality guru around to all of your customers to help them get certified. Remember, the healthier your customers are, the healthier you will be. Effective public relations will get you much better visibility at only a fraction of the cost. Next, think about further merchandising your achievement by placing your registration mark on your literature, business cards, invoices, and company letterhead. Do not put the registration mark on your product. Certification is a "good housekeeping" seal for your business and in no way infers product fitness (in fact, you can lose your certification for such an offense). In addition, don't forget to train your sales force on what ISO 9000 is and prepare them to answer questions and show the certificate. Did you ever hear of a CEO that didn't want to hear about how to make significant improvements in corporate performance? When used properly, ISO 9000 could make the difference between your sales force gaining access to the executive suite over your competition.

Customer Perception

Tom Peters, in his book, *Thriving on Chaos*, describes the results of the PIMS (Profit Impact of Market Strategy) study, conducted by the Strategic Planning Institute (Cambridge, MA). This study found that high market share provides profits, however, long-term market share comes from "perceived product or service quality." Perceived means as seen through the customers' eyes rather than the producers'. The study also found that changes in quality have a significantly greater effect on market share than price.

In James Sewel's book, *Customers For Life*, the author illustrates how effective the concept of perceived quality can be when coupled with a structured system for customer satisfaction. He presents the results of a study in which a Cadillac dealership with a focus on service and customer perception is compared with Cadillac dealers nationwide, demonstrating how two identical cars can be perceived completely differently. The following table illustrates the percentage of customers who indicated they would purchase the same make:

	One Dealer	Nationwide
Definitely	47%	35%
Probably Not	9%	13%
Definitely Not	3%	9%

It can cost up to five times more to win a new customer than it does to keep an existing one. Sewel's example demonstrates a remarkable advantage over the other Cadillac dealers as well as other manufacturers of similar vehicles. A Gallup poll asked what people were willing to pay for a product that they perceived as having higher than average quality. The results were:

- Approximately 30% more for a better car.
- Approximately 50% more for a better household appliance.
- Approximately 200% more for a better low-price personal item.

Sewel's results, combined with the Gallup poll, clearly demonstrate the business need to generate high levels of perceived quality for your company and its products. ISO 9000 certification offers a clear, readily understandable criterion for evaluation.

ISO 9000 has become the base quality standard for the U.S. The American National Standards Institute (ANSI) has adopted ISO 9000 and has renamed it as the Q90 series in 1990. As certification to the standard becomes more common, your customers will use it as a means of evaluation. If you can demonstrate certification, you will save your customer the cost of evaluation and it will also reduce your costs as customer audits go down. You can spend more time with your customers developing products or helping them figure out how you can both reduce your cycle times and total costs.

When will this happen? Will it become a U.S. requirement as well as a European one? There is no easy answer, but we believe it will be soon. If the experience in the U.K. is any indicator, it took about a year for the awareness to grow and for certification to begin for the BS 5750 code. Before it became an EC adopted standard, growth was consistent at about 50% per year, as seen in Figure 3.4. We would expect that the U.S. would see at least the same growth rate given the European requirement and the growing domestic awareness. According to Mark Morrow, editor of *Quality Systems Update*, a newsletter dedicated to the issues associated with ISO 9000 (Figure 3.5), hundreds of companies are now on the threshold of receiving certification and the number of certified

U.S. owned facilities will quadruple in the next year. A listing of certified facilities in the U.S. and Canada has been compiled by *Quality Systems Update,* as shown in Figure 3.6.

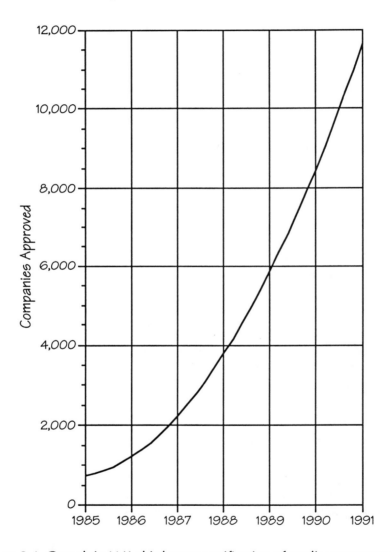

Figure 3.4 Growth in U.K. third-party certification of quality management systems. Source: Det Norske Veritas.

Quality Systems Update

An International Forum and Information Service

Volume II, Number 8   August 1992

US Figure Almost Doubles in Five Months

ISO 9000 Registered Company Sites: 400 in US; 201 in Canada

Four hundred United States company sites are registered to the ISO 9000 quality system standard, according to the latest figures gathered by *Quality Systems Update*. The number of registered sites represents a nearly 80-percent increase in US registrations in only five months.

The poll of European, US and Canadian registrars found 201 Canadian company sites registered to the ISO 9000 series standard. This is the first time *QSU* has published information on the number of Canadian registrations.

In February, 225 US sites were registered to the ISO 9000 series standard. The increase in the number of registered companies represents 175 newly issued certificates from February to July. It does not mean that the companies began and ended registration efforts during the five-month period.

BSi, QMI Lead Registrars

British Standards Institute Quality Assurance (BSi QA) and Quality Management

Institute (QMI) lead by a good margin in the number of registrations awarded in the US and Canada, respectively. BSi has issued a quarter of all US registrations, while QMI has performed all but 20 of the registration audits for Canadian companies. BSi has registered 101 of the 400 US-registered companies, while QMI has awarded registration certificates to 181 of 201 Canadian-registered companies. (See charts, page 7-8).

Curiously, more than 70 percent of the registrations awarded in Canada have been for ISO 9003, while only four percent of US registrations have been granted for that standard, the least comprehensive of the ISO 9000 series.

Bill Zub of QMI said many Canadian companies are registered to ISO 9003, the standard for final inspection and test, because they are distributors for parent companies located elsewhere. Zubb said the Canadian companies oftentimes pursue a joint registration to Canadian standard Z299.3

(continued on page 7)

Denmark's Reticence to Approve Maastricht Treaty Does Not Affect Technical Standard Integration

Denmark's recent refusal to adopt the European Economic Community's (EEC) treaty will have no effect on the timetable for the adoption of common technical standards including the ISO 9000 series (See Quality Forum for related article.).

According to EC experts, Denmark's disagreement with the EEC relates to questions of political and fiscal union. Common technical standards are supported by a separate document, *Completing the Internal Market, White Paper from the Commission to the European Council. Com (85) 310 final at 3 (June 14. 1985)]*.

The White Paper does not deal with political issues such as sovereignty, monetary integration, the taxing power of member states or military integration. Instead it is a clear, concise technical statement put forth by the EC Commission. It contains approxi-

mately 300 pieces of legislation for adoption and a clear timetable.

Paper Purposes

EC expert Jim Kolka points out that the White Paper is a perfect working document for standards development. The Commission limited its scope to concerns that member states already had acknowledged formally

(continued on page 11)

Figure 3.5 As the events and issues associated with ISO 9000 unravel, Quality Systems Update keeps you up-to-date with the latest developments.

Figure 3.6 *This directory of certified companies within the U.S. and Canada, published and updated by* Quality Systems Update, *will allow a purchasing agent to quickly determine whether your company or manufacturing site has been certified to the ISO 9000 standard.*

Internal Organizational Health

Remember, ISO 9000 ensures that a foundation for good business practice is in place. It also forces a linkage between organizations and improves communications. ISO 9000 will cause a gradual improvement in your operation as it requires implementation of a corrective action process. However, it adds a major competitive advantage in its support of your overall quality improvement program, that is, the profitable growth part. This foundation will allow you to meet the challenge of true quality:

Quality is exceeding your customer's expectations while maintaining profitable growth.

This quality definition can be further broken down to the "seven P's." You need all seven to consistently exceed your customer's expectations and the P's are supported by ISO 9000 as well.

1. Product performance to customers' specification.
2. Perception by customers that needs are exceeded in all areas.
3. Progressive improvement of performance
   (to meet growing customer expectations).
4. Process stability as a foundation for speed and accuracy.
5. Profitability that allows further investment and growth.
6. People empowerment
   (the driving force for meeting customer expectations).
7. Partnership (customers and suppliers).

ISO 9000 has far-reaching implications beyond procedures and documentation. Conformance will not only get you onto the global playing field, but it will also effect positive organizational change, improve your competitive position, enhance your company's market perception, and ultimately improve your bottom line. The choice is yours.

4

The Road To Discovery

For most companies, ISO 9000 will either augment ongoing quality efforts or spark a renewed emphasis on quality. This chapter will describe the events surrounding the certification process of the Foxboro Company, an 85-year-old New England manufacturer of measurement instruments and systems for process automation, to ISO 9001. Like many manufacturers today, the Foxboro Company had to adjust its paradigms for business in the 1990s. ISO 9000 played a major role in achieving this adjustment.

Among the First to Achieve ISO 9000 Certification

The Foxboro Company develops, manufactures, engineers, and integrates control systems, analytical instruments, and sensing and control devices for the process industries. Its products measure and automate processes in industries such as pulp and paper, oil refining, utilities, pharmaceuticals, food products, mining, and steel production. Foxboro was a Fortune 500 company through September 1990, when it was purchased by Siebe plc, a U.K.-based engineering and controls company traded on the London Stock Exchange.

The Foxboro Company was one of the first companies in the United States to become fully certified to ISO 9001. A short time later, its joint-venture manufacturing plant in the People's Republic of China became certified to ISO 9001, making it the first company to achieve any form of ISO 9000 certification in the P.R.C. While Foxboro has aggressively pursued ISO 9000, the real story is the role ISO played in the turnaround of the company's quality efforts. The following story is a tribute to the employees of The Foxboro Company — their collective efforts were instrumental in achieving ISO 9001.

Evolution to ISO 9000

At Foxboro, we are first to admit that we don't have all the answers, nor do we believe we will ever get to that point. After more than three years into our TQM journey, we realize that we have just begun.

We learned from our initial World Class Manufacturing (WCM) lessons that process stability is critical for success, and we applied this knowledge across the entire enterprise. What started out as a WCM effort has grown to become a World Class Enterprise (WCE) effort with ongoing positive results.

A few years ago, a cartoon by Gary Larson of *The Far Side* described Foxboro's situation in the mid-1980s. It pictured a dinosaur behind a podium addressing a conference of dinosaurs, with the caption, "The picture's pretty bleak, gentlemen... the world's climates are changing, the mammals are taking over, and we all have a brain about the size of a walnut." We were experiencing dramatic change. Unless we began to focus and use our intelligence, we would have suffered the same fate.

In the 1960s and 1970s, Foxboro was the dominant player in the process control industry; our margins were good, and the world was our oyster — as it seemed for many companies. In the midst of our success, we became complacent and failed to notice that the climate was rapidly changing. We suddenly encountered new domestic and foreign competitors who were aggressive and hungry. We watched our business environment deteriorate, and, for quite a while, we just tried to wish it away. Our first major restructuring occurred in 1985 followed by another in 1987. Even after we began our Total Quality journey at Foxboro, we continued to pay the price for our earlier lack of responsiveness. If employee population is a measure of pain, ours was significant. Our employment plummeted from a high of 12,000 in 1985 to its current level of 4,000. Yet today we ship roughly three times more per employee than we did in 1985. Although it is sad to see the departure of so many people, the future for those remaining is very bright.

In 1987, the Touche Ross consulting group asked the Foxboro Company to participate in an industry-wide study to identify the factors critical for a company to achieve World-Class status. The group benchmarked various automation suppliers to determine the critical factors for success. The results made it clear that Foxboro would need to embrace the following principles if we were to survive:

> There will be no safe harbor from the onslaught of competition — we were already witnessing the wave. No industry is secure, however, as is shown by the crippled giants of the past.

> Thresholds for performance will continually increase. The strong capabilities of today will become the mediocre performances of tomorrow. Process capabilities must improve, and speed will determine the winners.

> The leaders in the market will dictate the standards. If we seize the lead, we can set the standards that would cause our competitors to follow. If you aren't the leader, your profits will reflect your "me too" status.

> To remain viable you must always attempt to exceed the new standards, realizing that it takes time to get there, and by the time you do achieve your goal, the standard probably will have grown to meet your improvement.

> Quality will be the number one requirement for customer satisfaction in the 1990s.

> Quality is to be defined by our customers, regardless of what we believed. Our customers will point the way. Those companies that are able to maintain a close relationship with their customers will gain the greatest

understanding of their requirements, and in turn, will have the opportunity to produce the best product for the customer first. Those companies that are able to demonstrate conformance to their customers' standards will enjoy market share.

We now believe that ISO 9000 certification is a conformance standard that our friends at Touche Ross were foretelling. We use these guidelines and are aggressively communicating our position and commitment to this quality issue to our customers. Being one of the first companies to meet this hurdle demonstrates our commitment to them. Quality has become one of our weapons, and we are determined to continue to improve.

The competitive benchmarking efforts reinforced the need to improve our competitive position. As we were conducting our survey with Touche Ross, our customers were also beginning to give us signals that indeed the climate had changed and we were looking at extinction if we did not migrate toward quality. The following is just one example.

TQM Recognized

As mentioned in a previous chapter, in 1979, the Ford Motor Company recalled more cars than it produced. At that time, Dr. Deming advised Ford of the need for process integrity and the need to get its suppliers involved. He pointed out that unless it could control its processes, all of its other efforts would be in vain. When Ford's customers sat inside a Ford vehicle they actually saw Ford's suppliers, in this case, the suppliers of upholstery and carpeting. Deming said that these suppliers had to deliver a quality product and continually improve their product simultaneously with Ford. The supplier as well as Ford needed to have an active quality program.

The only way a company could ensure a high-quality product was to select high-quality suppliers of materials and tools. This meant a supplier that not only produced a high-quality product, but did so consistently. Suppliers who met this objective would enjoy Ford's business.

Ford took the initiative with its "Quality is Job #1" program. Ten years later, Ford is still advertising it. Ford also took Dr. Deming's advice and went to its suppliers; in this case, the supplier of fabrics was told to put together a quality program that would deliver a quality product coming from a quality process focused on continuous improvement. That supplier later went on to win the Baldrige Award.

As shown in Figure 4.1, Ford told the supplier it wanted consistent color and a fabric that would last for the life of the car. The fabric supplier also recognized that raw material consistency was the key to its success. It could not produce consistent color or keep the threads from breaking without robust and consistent raw materials. The supplier, in turn, went to its raw material supplier and restated Ford's requirements. The raw material supplier certainly did not want to lose one of its customers, so it cooperated and set up a quality program as well. As it was establishing a quality program, it quickly discovered the lessons learned at Ford and began to work with its own suppliers.

Enter Foxboro, the supplier that provided the equipment that controlled the process used to manufacture the raw materials. The message was the same all the way down the supplier chain. "Get your process under control, focus on continuous improvement, implement a Total Quality Management program, or get out!" At that point in time, however, things were not all well at Foxboro:

• New product development was not keeping ahead of the competition.
• Waste and yields were not being aggressively pursued.
• We launched a "bet the company" product prematurely.
• Deliveries across all product lines were unreliable.
• Our customer satisfaction was at an all-time low.

In late 1987, one of Foxboro's vice-presidents was called down to the raw material manufacturer and told to either get a quality program or look for a new customer. Adding this to what we had heard earlier from Touche Ross, Foxboro responded in a classic, knee-jerk fashion, "let's go out quickly and buy a program." On a Friday, we bought a quality

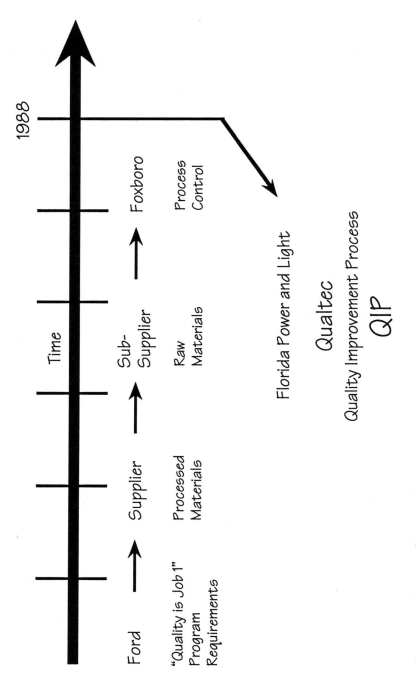

Figure 4.1 Origins of TQM at The Foxboro Company.

module from one quality consultant, and by the following Tuesday, we purchased an entirely different program from another quality practitioner. But we got lucky. The program we finally settled on, QIP (Quality Improvement Process) from Qualtec Quality Services, Inc. (a Florida Power and Light company), has satisfied our needs and served us well (see Figure 4.2).

QIP met our cultural and financial needs, it was supported by Qualtec (an outside agency that could provide constancy), it was modular and structured for easy deployment in our organization, and most important, our senior management was behind it, thereby, providing the management constancy needed to make it succeed. QIP has become one key ingredient in Foxboro's TQM program.

The practice of this quality improvement process contributed to Florida Power and Light's winning of the prestigious Japanese Deming Award. With a purchased program and a consultant in hand, we embarked on our quest for quality improvement.

QIP is a long-term strategy for influencing a positive financial performance. It involves a companywide focus on customer satisfaction.

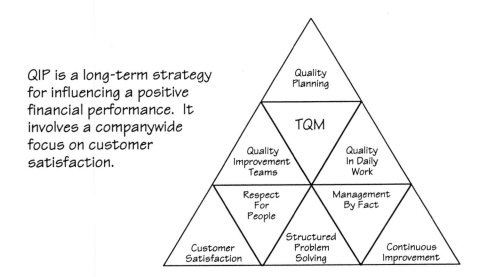

Figure 4.2 QIP at Foxboro based on Qualtec's program.

QIP at Foxboro

Foxboro's QIP program, introduced in 1989, consists of five strategic elements.

1 • Customer Satisfaction–Take care of your customer. Determine their concerns, make sure you can fix them, and begin working on it.

2 • Management by Fact – The only way to run a business; gut feelings don't count.

3 • Structured Problem Solving – Use a structured problem-solving process that focuses on the root cause of a problem, and then methodically implement upgrades that affect the root cause. "Band-Aid" approaches don't work — this process fixes long-term problems that have eluded quick fixes.

4 • Respect for People – It is no longer the person who postures and pounds fists that gets the respect. It's the individual who can build consensus within a group and empower employees to go out and satisfy customers. It's also those people who can cause constancy in an organization and make the group move quickly.

5 • Continuous Improvement – This is a mind-set that Henry Ford perfected and talked about in his book *Today and Tomorrow,* written in 1926. Once your employees realize that all jobs can be improved, it becomes a way of life and the defenses come down.

Foxboro employees are trained in these elements through their participation in QIP teams. Each team consists of five to seven employees who receive a week of training. In addition, each team has a Team Leader who is trained for an additional week and a Facilitator who is trained for three weeks. The team uses a structured problem-solving process, utilizing the statistical and analytical tools they have been trained on, and follows a storyboard approach, as seen in Figure 4.3.

The team focuses on a common customer and goes about addressing the "tall pole" problems — those few problems that cause the majority of the pain — that this customer is experiencing. The good news is that the teams solve long-term problems. The better news is that the team members take the training they have received back to their regular jobs.

Figure 4.3 Storyboard used with the QIP problem-solving process.

We have seen a steady growth in the number of teams and their benefit to the company. For example, when attending a meeting, it is rare not to see a PAL (Purpose, Agenda & Limit) enforcement of the QIP meeting rules of conduct. We are seeing a cultural change with more than 1,000 employees trained in the QIP process.

The QIP program and teams began in early 1989 with excellent growth and results; over 120 active teams currently participate. The contribution of the first 13 teams returned more than $1 million in very real savings while generating unmeasurable positive returns in customer satisfaction. QIP teams, however, are not a "do everything" tool. The QIP team storyboard approach solves long-term problems systematically, in a structured environment. The solutions are very effective, but it does not happen quickly, nor does it cause radical or rapid change. In addition, it is not the only method to achieve customer satisfaction. In fact, Mr. Crosby, the quality guru, warns of a single-solution approach; beware of the "Happy Meals" syndrome, where everything comes in a neat box.

In mid-1989, Foxboro's new Vice President of Manufacturing (now President) realized that we had to break out of our prior manufacturing paradigm, and quickly. To this end, he initiated the World Class Manufacturing Program to cause the change that has since grown into Foxboro's TQM program, as seen in Figure 4.4.

World Class Manufacturing (WCM)

Foxboro's program included many of the concepts found in Richard J. Schonberger's book, *World Class Manufacturing*, while recognizing that most of these concepts were not new and, in fact, can be traced back to Henry Ford. The program also adopted the beliefs of leaders like Deming, Juran, Crosby, Feigenbaum, and a host of contemporary Japanese experts.

For Foxboro, WCM was an empowerment program. If as an employee you were focused on any of the key components of the program and you were communicating with your fellow employees to assure everyone was coordinated, you were encouraged to pursue it.

External Customer Requirements

Being world class meant that we had to reexamine who our customers were. As it turned out they were not only the "end users," but also the sales people, customer engineering, and our distributors. Of course, manufacturing wasn't talking to any of them on a regular basis. Therefore, we sat down with each of these groups and asked what was important to them from a process perspective. The following paragraphs illustrate what they told us.

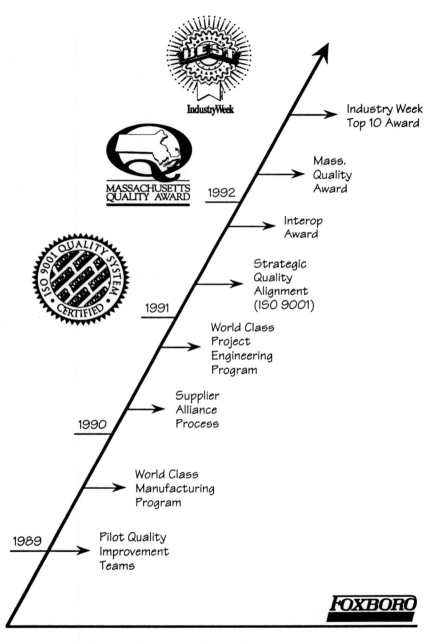

Figure 4.4 Evolution of TQM at The Foxboro Company.

Product – Reduce your variability; the product specification is just a minimum. One of the larger customers showed us the importance of product variability and how it impacts their operations. Delivering a product to specification was no longer good enough. We had to reduce the variability.

Delivery integrity – This was the most important measure of quality as expressed by our customers' buyers. The buyers are driven by two major factors. Did the product arrive on time? What is my purchase price variance? We realized we could never get beyond the buyers to sell our products if we did not perform on that first measure.

Process – They understand that if our processes exhibit a high level of process integrity (control), they are far more likely to receive a good product, on time, at the lowest total cost to them. In fact, our customers pointed out that we could not consistently deliver any of their requirements unless we had our processes under control. Here's the example they used. "Foxboro could send a salesperson in at $200 per call in expenses 50 times during a three-year period. It takes just one site inspection on our part to determine that your processes are not under control, making your $10,000 investment worthless. So, Foxboro, put your money into process integrity, then call on us."

Reduce your lead times – "In most cases, stay competitive but figure out a way we can obtain small quantities quickly. In some cases, we receive last minute changes to our order and need the response." This is critical to our distributors, because even though they stock products, they undergo surges and wanes. The more we make them wait, the more they have to stock, which incurs cost. This cost is borne by the end users, or worse, enjoyed by the competition.

Increase your flexibility – This is the improved ability to call out various configurations in modular combinations. They also spoke of flexibility in terms of delivery crisis. One of our customers had experienced a serious freeze that damaged their plant. They needed 250 instruments to get up and running, and of course this happened over the Christmas shutdown. In response to a desperate customer, Foxboro called in a large work force and had the instruments in the air within two days. No operation outside Foxboro could stock for that type of demand, and our customers depend on that capability.

Administration – A QIP team with a customer taught us something we had never really given much thought to. Even though our instrument price was less than our competitors, when the customer received the instrument and couldn't match it with the order paperwork, the customer spent $130 trying to reconcile the two, making our instrument more expensive. But, we were also told that if we could put the customer's inventory location and instructions on the upper right hand corner of the box, we could reduce the cost by $30, making our instrument much less expensive than our competitors'. This customer was looking at the *total cost* of doing business and realized that the purchase price was usually a small fraction of the Total Cost of Ownership. We also need to mention that not allowing our customers to easily match our invoices with material received frustrates their receiving operations, which is usually tied into the materials organizations (where the buyers are located). When they can't receive your material easily, they have a tendency not to pay you very quickly, which then puts pressure on your receivables department. They, in turn, further harass your customer for prompt payment and your relationship with your customer deteriorates.

New and improved products that support the lowest life-cycle cost – If we can invest in a product component that extends the mean-time-between-failure from 15 years to 30, we will do it. If we can produce a device that requires calibration only once a year versus twice, we will go ahead with the improvement, even if it does cost significantly more, because then our customer would have to bear the cost of sending out a crew to calibrate the instrument or replace it or possibly shut down an operation generating revenue at a rate of thousands of dollars per minute. Our customers are becoming very astute on the issue of total cost. The purchase price of a product is just a fraction of the total cost of a product.

Concurrent development – Our customers have unique competitive opportunities with limited windows to capture market share or where small savings can account for large earnings. A good supplier will quickly move with its customers to help them capture the opportunity and will develop a structured ongoing relationship that will support customers' needs. At Foxboro, that means not only a formal relationship with our customers, but a formal program to integrate our suppliers in the rapid development and delivery of new and competitive products. Simply, our customers were asking us to help them become more competitive — that's what it's all about. You won't be successful if your people don't know their roles and the system remains undefined. ISO 9000 compliance addresses the success of your organization because it addresses these two factors. Supporting these defined customer needs required us to restructure the way we planned and carried out our business. We looked to the visionaries and incorporated their messages.

Strategic Components

Foxboro put in place a series of strategic manufacturing endeavors that incorporated the concepts of Deming and Juran, as seen in Figure 4.5. One involved a cultural change toward quality by driving Management Constancy through the use of various councils focused on the weak areas cited by our customers.

We also developed a series of performance measures that focused on continual improvement of the process used to satisfy our customers and carried out programs that ensured that our employees were heard and became involved. This included training in structured problem solving, quality tools, and JIT/TQC methods that focused on the elimination of waste and promotion of customer satisfaction.

We began a series of process upgrades to simplify how business was conducted. Finally, we completed the model with a series of cost reduction activities again focused on the reduction of nonvalue-added activities and redundancies.

As these programs were progressing, we began to encounter organizational roadblocks. They weren't over the destination but rather the methods and the standards to be used to reach the destination. The individuals involved, all excellent in their respective fields, brought along

Figure 4.5 Strategic components of Foxboro's World Class Manufacturing program.

differing perspectives and experience. Fortunately, they all adhered to the one universal truth of managing a business—Customer Satisfaction.

It is not that any of these people aren't excellent in their professions; it's just that their environment, training, and past are different. There is no universal truth when it comes to managing a business, except one — Customer Satisfaction.

This truth got us back on track. Again our customers pointed us in the right direction, to the ISO 9000 standard. At about the same time, our own senior quality people began telling us about the standard and suggested this might be a solution.

We looked at ISO 9000 and discovered that it addressed our entire business. It defined standards and expectations while accommodating a wide range of organizations and their uniqueness.

The manufacturing quality council adopted the standard and began integrating it into the manufacturing operations. We soon saw it had far wider implications than just manufacturing improvement.

Supplier Alliance Program

The Supplier Alliance program was initiated to capture the benefits that can be derived from a group of excellent suppliers integrated into our organization.

Foxboro over the years had adopted the mind-set that somehow we had to build everything and had established an infrastructure and overhead to match that expectation. We were not inclined to integrate our suppliers and capture the speed and excellence they were capable of offering. While business was growing rapidly and competitive pressures were low, this strategy masked a poor manufacturing policy. Once competition intensified, however, the overhead and inefficiencies prevented us from moving quickly.

As we began the supplier integration, we recognized that it was necessary not only to change how we selected our suppliers, but also to change how we managed our side of the business. We have broken down the traditional supplier/buyer organization and migrated to a commodity team management style. Our suppliers are now managed according to a philosophy that requires that both parties win, and they are involved in mutual continuous improvement and waste-elimination activities. We have seen some spectacular returns in waste reduction, improvements in lead times and flexibility, and new product introductions.

We also believe that by assisting our suppliers with their efforts, we will both enjoy their success. As of this writing, we have trained more than 370 suppliers during two large ISO 9000 training sessions.

World Class Project Engineering

One of the direct benefits to come from our ISO 9000 preparation was the discovery of our "Work Breakdown Structure" (WBS) methodology for doing business within our project engineering operations. This is an example of how the ISO 9000 team sought the best way to conduct business and meet the requirements of the standard. We have four industry engineering groups, each of which ran its operations in a unique fashion. As the team went through the ISO 9000 preparation process, they discovered that one of the groups had a much better defined process and its customers seemed to be responding more favorably. The projects came in on time and the group seemed to have their projects under better control and yielding a consistently higher margin. This became the standard for all our industry engineering operations. Now all our engineering groups are using the standard, people are interchangeable, and we are now even using the same symbols. The result is on-time projects, happy customers, cost control, reusable engineering, and savings of more than $1 million per year by reducing waste.

The WBS, as seen in Figure 4.6, breaks down a customer's needs into distinct phases and identifies the tasks, responsibilities, resource needs, and costs within each phase, enabling you to deliver a project within budget and on time. This gives you a competitive advantage, as long as you communicate your ability to the customer.

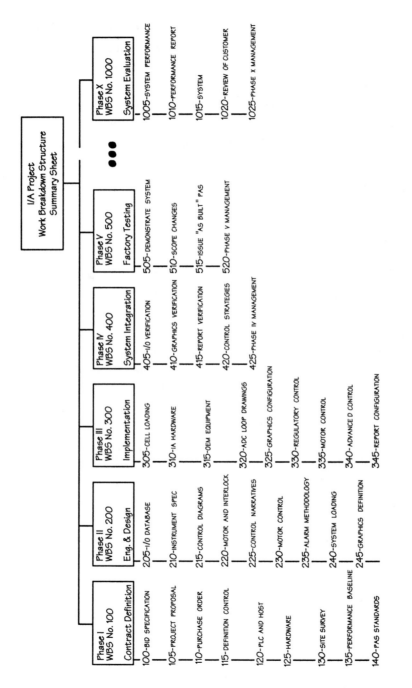

Figure 4.6　Work Breakdown Structure methodology used for world-class project execution.

Strategic Quality Alignment — Going for ISO 9001

Many positive programs were underway in the company. Real progress and positive results were being realized. But something was still missing. A common framework for running the business was needed that would not only provide a communications structure (procedures), but a means for transcending organizational boundaries to derive greater synergy among operations — in other words, a vehicle for creating a Strategic Quality Alignment of all our ongoing activities. The more we looked at and became aware of ISO 9000, we realized that it would provide the solution. We recognized that we needed to move ahead quickly for our own organizational health as well as to address the competitive issues described in the previous chapter.

We recognized that ISO 9000 would become a global standard and a basic minimum hurdle for doing business. We also expected to gain a competitive advantage by being one of the first to become certified. It would provide a visible example that Foxboro's quality approach was aggressive and committed to a Total Quality endeavor. As it turns out, it has also given us the opportunity to share our ISO 9000 certification experience with our customers. We regularly hold orientation and training sessions with them. It's cementing our relationship and in some cases putting our competitors in a defensive position.

The final and, in fact, the primary reason we began this journey was that of organizational health. We just knew it would make us a better company.

In March of 1991, we achieved what we term "Strategic Quality Alignment." This is significant not only because we became a fully certified company with the successful certification of all our domestic manufacturing operations (see Figure 4.7), but it was at that point that we had evolved our efforts into a working quality model. ISO 9000 certification was merely a milestone marker in our TQM journey.

A short time later, our joint-venture manufacturing plant in the People's Republic of China became certified to ISO 9001, making it the first company to achieve any form of ISO 9000 certification in the P.R.C. (see Figure 4.8).

Erkend door de Raad voor de Certificatie

Certificate No. QSC 1172

DET NORSKE VERITAS

QUALITY SYSTEM
CERTIFICATE OF CONFORMITY

This is to certify that the Quality System of:

THE FOXBORO COMPANY

I/A Plant & Neponset Plant, Massachusetts 02035 and Highland Plant, East Bridgewater 02333

has been found to conform to Quality System standard:

ISO 9001

This certification is valid for the following product/service ranges:

Design and Manufacturing of Process Control and Automation equipment.

Quality System Documentation: 57-000 13-64-1, 57-000 13-64-2, 57-000 13-64-3   Date: February 19 and 25, March 4, 1991

Audit Report : 57-000 13-64-01, 57-000 13-64-02, 57-000 13-64-03   Date: March 22, 1991

Period of validity April 4, 1991   to   April 4, 1994

The Certificate is not valid unless scheduled periodical audits have been performed in accordance with the Periodical Audit Plan No. QSC 1172

For Det norske Veritas

Management Representative
G.B. Castberg

Date: April 4, 1991

Lead Auditor
Ted M. Pankiw

Periodical Audits:

Per.Audit Report No.	-04, 05, 06 57-00013-64	57-00013-64-07 -08-09	57-00013-64- 10-11-12			
Date	Sept 29 1991	APR. 9, 1992	OCT. 13-16, 1992			
Lead Auditor Sign.	Q.E. Nudgren	Ted Pankiw	Ted Pankiw			

Figure 4.7 The Foxboro Company was one of the first major U.S. companies to achieve ISO 9001 certification.

Figure 4.8 The Foxboro Company was the first company to achieve any form of ISO 9000 certification in the People's Republic of China.

TQM: A Working Model

With our model in place, as shown in Figure 4.9, we have:
- A company being trained in five basic principles and tools via Qualtec's QIP team approach,
- Continuous improvement driven by quality teams. We support more than 120 QIP teams as well as the same number of less formal "Process Excellence Teams" (PETs) composed of groups such as World Class Manufacturing teams, Costs Reduction teams, JIT/TQC teams, DPU/ 2 teams, etc.
- We now have a tool, ISO 9000, that ensures a structured working environment that captures improvements and integrates them into a stable and structured operation, thereby keeping those good ideas from eroding.
- Finally, we have a management structure that actively supports and nurtures the model. It plans and executes around a matrixed decision

Figure 4.9 TQM: A working model.

and execution process. It promotes a working environment that respects and supports the employees who deliver Customer Satisfaction and Quality.

With a working model in place, we are able to support the structure with a series of drivers that translate the model into working vehicles. These drivers add guidance to the vehicles that carry the program into a series of actions creating the TQM climate focused on Customer Satisfaction and Quality.

At the end of the day, the real questions that must be asked are, what has all this done for our customers? How have we helped our customers?

TQM and ISO 9000 Benefits

As noted earlier, our customers asked for *delivery integrity* and *process stability.* They said they wanted us to *reduce waste* and the *total cost* of doing business with Foxboro. They needed a *quality product* that focused on their needs and that of their customers. The following are just some of the results we've realized as we move down the TQM path.

Delivery integrity – We are now in Baldrige winner country, but we aren't getting too carried away with our greater than 98% on-time figure (see Figure 4.10). We ship approximately 40,000 instruments and pieces of equipment every month. At 98% on-time we are still making 800 customers unhappy per month. While we have made progress, we still have a long way to go.

Plant inventories – In terms of waste reduction, we were able to cut our inventories in half. Henry Ford spends a lot of time in his book talking about inventory as waste. As we improved our processes, the inventory required was reduced, as seen in Figure 4.11. This was the equivalent of increasing sales by $60 million! Remarkably, at the same time, we improved delivery performance by 20%. Historically, inventory was perceived as an insurance policy against delivery shortfall.

4.10 Delivery Integrity (% On Time). Delivery integrity for all Foxboro products has improved significantly since the introduction of TQM.

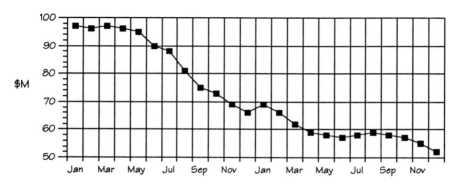

4.11 Inventory ($M). Total inventories have been reduced dramatically, contributing to waste elimination and cost reductions.

4.12 Product Cost Reductions ($M). TQM has played a major role in product cost reductions.

Material cost reductions – Total cost reduction takes many forms. In our systems manufacturing operations, we were able to trim our material cost by more than $4 million (see Figure 4.12). This was achieved by teams of employees getting together and looking at our products and seeing where they could make them better while reducing the costs. The ground rules are simple; cost reduction can only occur when the products' mean time between failure has been maintained or improved. We saved more than 5% in material costs across the company using this team-focused approach.

Employee involvement – We asked our employees in those areas where they traditionally were not subject to rigorous procedures and structure requirements what they thought of this effort. Their feedback is summarized below and listed in Figure 4.13:

We have consistency, not dependent on any one individual. – As you remove the redundancy from your organization and trim down, it becomes exceedingly important that people can step in for others, that they have been trained such that the operation doesn't come to a complete stop. It is also critical that the functions are all done in the same fashion and thus reduce variation. This occurred with one of our quality teams as we were installing our ISO 9000 program. This team was attempting to reduce defects occurring over a three-shift operation of a group that was only achieving a mid-60% yield on their finished product. The team looked at the problem and discovered that each operator on each shift performed the job differently. Each tweaked the equipment to what they thought produced the best product. As the materials moved through this operation, there were tremendous tolerance "stack-ups" resulting in a tremendous waste of materials. By having all three shifts develop and agree on a single machining and assembly methodology, the yields are now higher than 95%.

There is a home for good ideas. – This might be one of the most powerful aspects of ISO 9000, as employees only contribute when they know they will be heard.

Our performance indicators have improved. – Credit memos are down. While we pursued this model, we have reduced the quantity of

- Have procedures where none existed before.

- Everyone speaking the same language.

- We have consistency in operation...
  not dependent upon any one individual.

- There is a home for good ideas.

- The system is universal within the company.

- Have formalized the corrective action process.

- Our performance indicators are revealing highly positive results.

- Reduced product rework.

- We have early detection of potential design oversights.

- Improved team communications.

- Increased participation in design reviews.

Figure 4.13 TQM and ISO 9000 benefits as described by employees.

credits being written by 70%. A credit is the result of a mistake. This represents a saving of $200 to $300 for both Foxboro and our customers on each credit memo issued.

Improved team communication. —Employees know what is expected of them and this removes or reduces the defensiveness or squabbles that seemed to go along with events and ownership.

Increased participation in design reviews. —Employees now come to the meetings prepared and understand the expected outcomes of the meetings. The result of this process streamlining has surprised us. A significant event occurred after the process had been in place that validated the efforts. Our engineering staff took three multilayer printed circuit board schematics from drawings to working prototypes (multilayer board and surface mount components) onto a single panel with fully functional test points in two weeks, versus the more typical four to six months. If the requirement is speed, all involved employees simultaneously using practiced routines is the answer.

Beyond ISO 9000

ISO 9000 was certainly a significant event in the history of the Foxboro Company. In addition to the certificate, we achieved the objectives we set for process improvements and further improving our business methodologies.

With continuous improvement being one of our TQM cornerstones, we quickly evaluated what the next step in our journey should be, now that we had achieved strategic alignment with ISO 9000. We concluded that the Baldrige application was a future possibility. Its criteria provides an excellent means for evaluating our performance and provides a foundation for improvement. At about the same time, we learned that the state of Massachusetts had initiated the Armand Feigenbaum Massachusetts Quality Award based on the Baldrige criteria. We viewed the Massachusetts Quality Award as a good opportunity to do a "dry run" of the Baldrige and simultaneously take the next step in the journey. A year after receiving our ISO 9000 certification and many hours of preparation, we submitted our application for the award. A rigorous audit and six months later, we became one of the proud recipients of the first Armand Feigenbaum Massachusetts Quality Award in October of 1992 (see Figure 4.14).

Coincidentally, in October 1992, Foxboro was selected by *Industry Week* as having one of the top 10 plants in the U.S. as a part of their annual Best Plants awards (see Figure 4.15). The recognition we have received through the Massachusetts Quality Award and the *Industry Week* Top Ten Award provides benchmarks demonstrating that our pursuit of TQM, built on a strong ISO 9000 foundation, is on course.

4.14 Foxboro's TQM efforts enabled it to win the Armand Feigenbaum Massachusetts Quality Award based on the Baldrige criteria.

4.15 Foxboro's ISO 9001 certification and its TQM programs contributed to Industry Week *recognizing it as one of the top 10 plants in the U.S.*

The Bottom Line Is the Bottom Line

Our customers saw what we were doing and wanted to share in our methodologies and results. For example, we used a Foxboro QIP team with a team from an AMOCO operation. Through our joint efforts, we became the first certified "Distributed Controls" supplier for their Chocolate Bayou plant. While the team was one of the activities most visible to AMOCO, it was really the entire company coming together, as well as our distributors (Figure 4.16).

Our customers have responded favorably through their growing commitment to our products and services. Here is an example: while pulp and paper industry capital expenditures plummeted from roughly $17 billion to $10 billion between 1990 and 1991, our volume in this market grew by more than 15%!

THE FOXBORO COMPANY
FOXBORO, MASSACHUSETTS

IN RECOGNITION OF
THE ESTABLISHMENT OF
OUR QUALITY PARTNERSHIP.
BASED UPON SUSTAINED PERFORMANCE,
CONFORMANCE TO REQUIREMENTS,
DEMONSTRATED COMMITMENT,
AND CONTINUOUS IMPROVEMENT

AMOCO CHEMICAL COMPANY
CHOCOLATE BAYOU PLANT
ALVIN, TEXAS

HONORS THE FOXBORO COMPANY AS A
CERTIFIED QUALITY SUPPLIER ON OCTO-
BER 11, 1990

4.16 Through the efforts of a joint QIP team with AMOCO, Foxboro became the first company to achieve certified status for the supply of automation systems to the Chocolate Bayou Plant.

4.17 To help with their ISO 9000 pursuits, Foxboro provides regular training sessions for both its customers and suppliers.

This is what it is all about — helping our customers become more competitive by helping them directly — assisting them as they improve their process with our products and services, and sharing with them common challenges such as ISO 9000. Hopefully, we are saving them hundreds of hours so they can better serve their customers. Of course, that will mean more business for them and for us.

To help with their ISO 9000 pursuits, we hold regular training sessions for both our customers and suppliers (Figure 4.17). We average two to three customer training sessions per month. We know they appreciate our efforts — we are using our quality organization to meet our definition of quality: "To exceed our customers expectations while maintaining profitable growth."

5

How Will We Ever Be Ready In Time?

Qualifying for and receiving certification is an enterprisewide endeavor. Even with management commitment and an existing quality infrastructure in place, it can take anywhere from three months to one year to mobilize your operations and get the proper documents, procedures, internal audits, and practices in place.

This chapter presents a sample project schedule and describes the events leading up to a certification audit, based on the experiences of the Foxboro Company.

How Long Will It Take?

The following time frames for certification are suggested; they assume a single plant operation and management commitment.

3 to 6 months	If you are in full compliance to a military standard or nuclear standard.
6 to 10 months	If your organization has fairly up-to-date procedures, job descriptions, and a working quality organization.
10 to 16 months	If the organization has only sketchy procedures and its records are haphazard. Your quality organization is still responsible for final inspection, and still takes the blame for the substandard product shipped. If you have a very large plant site.

16 to 24 months   If you still don't have full commitment from
                       senior management. You shouldn't begin
                       your countdown until your management
                       commits to pursuing certification.

Most operations are focused on immediate problems, such as revenue and profits. Our survey of companies that achieved ISO 9000 early indicates that until there is a "stake" in the ground and people can see it coming, little motivation exists and the experience can be very frustrating for those trying to generate any meaningful effort.

The next section contains 14 steps that will enable you to measure your progress, as well as to estimate when you will be able to entertain the auditors with a world-class operation that is fully compliant with ISO 9000. A sample project schedule is illustrated in Figure 5.1.

How Much Will It Cost?

The cost of ISO 9000 compliance depends on the existing condition of your organization. Most certified companies have not tracked the costs. As discussed earlier, the value to the business far outweighs the cost, so tracking these costs is a nonvalue-added activity as long as your operation stays within its planned operating budget. One company's postaudit study showed a nine-month return on investment. Again it is a function of your current status, but the greater the opportunity for improvement, the greater the opportunity for return.

When Foxboro's plant managers were first told of the plan for the upgrade of the procedures, you can imagine it was not widely welcomed. Their first question was, "Where is the budget and what is the account number to dump these costs into?" The vice-president of manufacturing recognized this activity as part of running a good business and responded by saying, "Don't ask for something that you should have been doing already. If you can't get the QC engineers to participate, we will get new engineers. If you can't get the supervision to participate, we will get new supervision. If I can't get my plant managers to participate," he stopped

Figure 5.1 Sample project schedule illustrating the major steps undertaken by The Foxboro Company to achieve certification.

there and looked around the room and continued, "Need I say any more?" That took care of the cost issues as well as senior-level commitment.

The 14 Steps

The following is a description of the process that will help you achieve compliance and certification quickly. This is one approach. You should try to create your own plan tailored to your situation.

1 • Senior Management Commits – The old adage that commitment must come from the top holds true. Senior management must commit to achieving ISO 9000 compliance with a firm determination to achieve the objective, allocate the necessary resources, and assign responsibility appropriately. ISO 9000 is an enterprisewide standard that requires the shared commitment and involvement of all the executives within the senior management group and their respective operations. Remember this is not a "free lunch"; sacrifice is required for this commitment. Your organization has two choices: It can fund an outside consultant with a staff of writers or it can slow down other projects and perform the task with internal people who are close to the process and can usually do a much better job than an outsider. Should you decide to go internally, your management must keep in mind during the process that this is not business as usual; a strong commitment is needed.

At Foxboro, we let our employees and supervisors determine what would slow down. As long as it did not interfere with delivery integrity, their recommendation was generally accepted. Their only requirement was to tell us what would give.

Once you have senior management commitment, actively use it. Ask your plant managers to put ISO 9000 at the top of each staff meeting. This way it will not get lost in the agenda, and putting it first will send a clear message to the staff. Declare your intentions throughout the entire organization, with a letter of commitment from the senior person in the organization. That commitment will serve you well, and, without it, your chances for success are significantly reduced.

2 • Establish an ISO 9000 Steering Council – The primary charter of this council is to establish a comprehensive ISO 9000 development program and ensure its implementation with the proper allocation of resources. This group functions as the focal point for all the activities within the organization related to ISO 9000. They will provide the comprehensive assessments necessary for scheduling and supporting the audit. They will be negotiating tasks and interfaces within their own organization as the project leaders, as well as between organizations for linkages.

Recognize that ISO 9000 is an enterprisewide effort when putting this council together, and that everyone must be involved. Even if you are preparing for ISO 9002, be sure to include representatives from all organizations that intersect the certified areas. When you go to your senior management for representatives, ask for the best. Remind them that these people will be representing them and committing their organizations to plans of action. Remind them that they do not want to be the organizational group that causes the company to fail (that reminder seems to be effective in areas that are not completely committed). Make sure the people assigned to the committee are your best performers. Although it seems that they can't be spared for the task, you need the best. Once they are on the team, remind their managers that this is not a free ride — they should work with their designate to free up some of his or her time and see that recognition is received for this work. With the good performers on your team, you will notice that they receive peer support that will make accomplishment of the overall mission easier. One of the first tasks should be the education of the council.

3 • Educate the Council on ISO 9000 – It is critical that the council members understand ISO 9000 and its elements in detail, as they will champion the effort in their respective organizations. It is also important that they develop a consensus among themselves as to what ISO 9000 is within their organization. To assist in their efforts, questionnaires developed by the various certifying agencies should be obtained and used to assess organizational readiness. One that is commonly used is the UL certification questionnaire (RP-2: Facility Survey Form; it is not clear that Underwriters Lab will readily provide this document and if so at what cost). The education of the steering committee will create a group of roving experts, who are also self-reinforcing drivers with the ability to move the process forward quickly. People generally don't want to put work into something for which they don't understand the reason, especially if they would rather be doing something else. If your team can convey the purpose of the effort and provide correct and timely answers to questions, they will motivate the other employees to join the effort. Conversely, not providing answers will stall the effort.

4 • Evaluate and Select a Certification Agent – The evaluation and selection of a certification agent is critical and should be viewed as a marriage between two parties. Thus, you will want to look very closely at the likely partners. The following is a checklist of things to consider when you go through your search for a certification partner:

- Your certification audit should not be the first time you meet your auditors. Plan on spending some time "courting" your auditors.
- Does this potential partner need to carry a recognized European registration mark?
- Is the potential partner local or will this be a long-distance relationship? Don't dismiss a long-distance relationship if the partner seems right, but involves an extra cost. Try to find out what the costs are, including their application fees, initial visit costs, the certification audit costs and expenses, cost of future get togethers, and cancellation fees.
- Is the potential partner your type? Do they know about your type of business, and can they talk your language? Do you have the same interests (authorized to grant certification to your type of business), have they worked with other people in your line of business, and can they give you a reference in your industry to call?
- What kind of friends does the agency keep? Do they have MOU's (Memorandums of Understanding) with other registration organizations that recognize the others' certification, for example, UL and BSI. Be careful as there are different levels of MOU's. The following are four common MOU's.[1]

---

[1] Catherine Neville, General Manager, QMI.

- A *Bilateral Agreement* says we unconditionally accept the other's certificate .
- A *Full MOU* means we still accept the other's certificate, but every so often we would like to view the audits.
- A *Developing MOU* means that we have agreed to look at each other very closely and may honor each other's certificate in the future.
- A *Base MOU* means that we have agreed to agree at some time in the future.

When the agent's MOU claims sound too good to be true, they are. Ask for details and type. Clearly the more the better, but don't discount them if they only have a few.

- Is the agency available? When you call, do they speak with you or pass you around? Do they meet the 48-hour return-your-call test? Can they meet with you for an introductory chat? Can they specify when they could perform the certification audit?
- Is the agency expensive? Don't be misled by an artificially low initial quote with the intention of accelerating the meter later. They are all fairly competitive; however, be leery of the "two people, two days" quote. Respect the person who might want to go to a place where you can talk and enjoy yourselves; that's how good relationships are built.
- Now, for the most important question: Do you like each other? Do they approach you with a positive attitude — one that indicates they want to make it a positive experience for both, that they are really interested in your making the grade? They realize that you may be a bit nervous and are open and patient with your exploring questions, and they respond quickly and accurately to your inquiries. Your questions may be similar to the following ones:

How often will you stop by and visit? Some certifiers visit every six months, others only once a year. There are advantages and disadvantages either way.

How long in advance will you call before you come? Some certifiers lay out a three-year schedule and allow you to look and be your best when they get there. Others call only two weeks before they plan to arrive. While this can be very uncomfortable, especially if you have a busy schedule or a full house of customers, it is palatable, but rarely can you look and feel your best. Don't assume that you can only spruce up just before they get there — they know how to get an accurate reading regardless of your preparation.

How do they look at the world? Some certifiers only see black or white, pass or fail, when they score you after the certification audit. Others see shades of passing or failing and give a range of scores. They will all ask the same kinds of questions and look in the same 400 places if you are going after ISO 9001. Our evaluation considered the "pass/fail" approach undesirable. We wanted to know how we were doing for two reasons:

1. We wanted to use this as an exercise for improvement and would first focus on our weaker areas. Pass/fail would not provide that information.

2. If we didn't know where we were marginal, it was unlikely that we would discover it prior to their reaudit. You just know that they are going to look first where the result on the last audit was marginal.

What if we don't pass on the first try of the certification audit? It depends on how badly you missed the points and where. Each certifier has a different approach. One may say, "we will be back within 30 days" and then will only look at your shortfalls, provided they weren't major points. At the other extreme, another may say, "don't hold your breath," meaning that you're back to square one. Ask, and be sure to negotiate a follow-up date once you have set up the agreement for the first audit, just in case you don't make it the first time.

What's the family like? Are the siblings capable of being quiet about what they might overhear; how can you be sure? You want to make sure that the registrar has confidentiality agreements with its employees and all who would see your audit information.

ISO 9000 is an interpretive standard and, therefore, has gray areas. Try to find a certification agent that understands your business. Get to know the probable lead auditor and find out the interpretation of some of the questions that you might not be able to resolve. This will allow you to calibrate your initial approach to the lead auditor's expectations. In addition, make it clear to your agency that you want someone who knows your industry's practices and "common sense."

Confirm that your certifier is financially sound, and scout out how their auditors were trained and who they work for. Some registrars actually out-source the audits to independent agencies, and you have to ask yourself whether that is in your best interest. You also want to make sure the auditors have been trained to a standard such as ASQC's Certified Quality Auditor standard.

If I should pass the certification audit, how can I announce it to the world? You need to find out not only exactly how you can inform your customers, but how they will be informing other certification agencies. In most cases, you are placed in a registry where customers and competitors alike can look you up. Hopefully, it is easily accessible. Your registrar should also have your announcement placed in directories like the *Quality Systems Update, Registered Company Directory for the United States and Canada*, as discussed in the previous chapter.

5 • *Define Quality Responsibility* – After the ISO Steering Council has been educated, begin the process of clearly defining the responsibility for quality and the associated processes, from the president down through the entire organization. The definition of responsibility does not necessarily indicate that the individual has to be dedicated solely to quality full time; however, it does mean the organization has to demonstrate that an individual is actively involved in the quality management of a particular process and has that specific responsibility. This includes documented proof that there has been an activity associated with the defined responsibility. This may sound fairly easy and, surprisingly, it is. Start by laying out a rough flow chart of your organization with your steering council, and then have each of the ISO 9000 team's members identify where their organization is affected by the standard. After they determine their areas of responsibility, have them sit with the other members for a review. You might discover that you're responsible for more than you think, or that some people think they have responsibilities that you think you have, or that no one has responsibility for certain areas. In any case, this can have ramifications beyond the scope of your council. If so, don't mess around, go to the top, explain your problem, ask for direction, and make it clear why it is so critical. Also ask for a decision date. This exercise accomplishes two tasks:

1. It becomes the basis for your quality manual.
2. It is a basic step in defining how your organization satisfies its customers — you now know who is doing what.

To assist the auditors, you will want to create an organization chart that will support your definition of how the responsibility flows. This will become the basis for your corporate-level quality manual and probably looks just like your current organization chart (just be sure the titles match your description of those responsible).

6 • Establish Procedure Structure – Before you start writing procedures, your group should determine the format of the procedures, as well as the best and most efficient method for maintaining this structure once it is established. This structure is the area that will require the greatest effort in preparation for the audit, and it will have a significant impact on your long-term procedural maintenance efficiency, so it deserves significant thought and effort.

A possible strategy would be to develop three (or two for a single plant) layers of procedures. A few, relatively stable procedures reside at the top of this structure, and the vast number of dynamic procedures reside at the lower levels. This approach minimizes the number of procedures and dramatically reduces the maintenance and coordination requirements.

In this layered structure, as seen in Figure 5.2, the top or corporate level is relatively general and primarily focused on the various standards that are being supported, how to approach ISO 9000 requirements, and the definition of the corporate quality assurance responsibilities. It should be brief.

The next level would cover plant or group-level procedures. They would define common elements and practices stated at the corporate

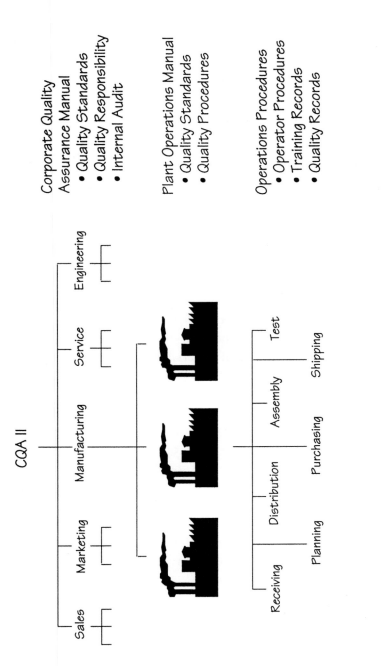

Corporate Quality
Assurance Manual
• Quality Standards
• Quality Responsibility
• Internal Audit

Plant Operations Manual
• Quality Standards
• Quality Procedures

Operations Procedures
• Operator Procedures
• Training Records
• Quality Records

CQA II

Sales   Marketing   Manufacturing   Service   Engineering

Receiving   Distribution   Assembly   Test

Planning   Purchasing   Shipping

Figure 5.2 Example of a hierarchial procedure structure used by The Foxboro Company.

level, and describe in greater detail the elements that relate to them.

The third and final level, departmental operations, is where detailed procedures, documents, and records are maintained. The majority of the detailed procedures reside at this level as well as in the department where they are being used.

It is likely that your existing quality procedures will need to be restructured. At a minimum, you will need to reference these procedures to the specific elements of the ISO 9000 standard to which they relate.

There is no one correct method for writing the actual procedure. We recommend that you allow each organization to generate the procedures in the fashion with which they are most comfortable. The steering committee should set a framework for minimum requirements of contents, and then let the groups decide what works best for them. The framework should require at least a date of issuance, revision number, location for use, an ISO 9000 reference number, and a procedure name. Acceptable procedures that are already in place can be used, as long as it can be ensured that they meet the framework. Procedures can take many forms. Most often, we see a playscript format. Sometimes a flow chart format works the best. They can be in an electronic database or in paper form. They can be on the backs of material transfer forms. They can be signs on the wall or even copies of the operating instructions that came with the equipment with an added cover page for control. Let the groups be creative in how they solve *their* problem. The more hurdles you put in front of them, the slower their progress will be.

As these procedures are being written, opportunities for standardization and replication in common areas shouldn't be missed. You will want to establish a structure that can readily uncover these common areas before beginning, and avoid a lot of unnecessary duplication. One strategy is to define general procedures simply and then break out only the necessary details according to the organizations they represent. This way, procedures will be relatively general at the higher levels and only get into detail as required at the lower levels.

You will also want to establish measures for progress. The number of outstanding procedures to be written is one measure that you can suggest to the groups as an indicator of progress. Before you get started, you will also need to define other requirements to ensure that the procedures incorporate all the critical ISO 9000 requirements.

7 • Define Documentation Standards – In this phase, the steering council must define and clarify all the documents required by the ISO 9000 standard. They should also identify as many of the commonly used documents as possible to save work for the organization.

Divide the documents that need to be defined and proceduralized among the team members to work on. Then prototype these documents in a single area and once the problems are removed, get the council to endorse them. Have each member go out to his or her area and do the installation. They may make their own adjustments, and that's OK, as long as they stay within the framework and document it to meet the standard. Attempt to make one document serve as many purposes as possible.

The following is a listing of the documents that must be generated and the records that must exist to support the standard.

Documentation
- Quality Policy and Objectives   (4.1.1)
- Quality Manual   (4.2 Note a)
- Design Control   (4.4)
- Work Instructions   (4.9.1)
- Final Inspections   (4.10.3)
- Instrument Calibration   (4.11.c)
- Nonconformities   (4.13)
- Corrective Actions   (4.14)
- Handling, Storage, Packing, Delivery   (4.15)
- Internal Quality Audits   (4.17)

System Records
- Management Review   (4.1.3)
- Subcontractors Assessment   (4.6.2)
- Instrument Calibration   (4.11.f)
- Audit Records   (4.17)
- Training   (4.18)

Contract/Product Records
- Contract Review (4.3)
- Design Verification (4.4.5.a)
- Product Identification (4.8)
- Inspection, Testing (4.10.4)
- Product Release (4.12)
- Nonconforming Products (4.13.1)

Because it is your business, the standard must be interpreted according to how you conduct your operations. For example, a company that sells catalog items will maintain a different set of contract records than one that builds nuclear power plants. Assembly documentation doesn't have to be a drawing; it can be a photo or a prototype with a part number written on it. The only requirement is that you control these drawings/photos/models to ensure that the proper item is being built at the right time and being tested properly.

It is impossible in the space of this book to cover all the conceivable methods for addressing these requirements. We would, however, like to briefly cover a few of the items here that won't be addressed later:

Quality Manual–Contrary to popular belief, the ISO 9000 standard does not state that you must have a quality manual, but we haven't seen any effective way to go through the process without one. The quality manual represents the focal point for your plan to run the business. Consider making this manual as "auditor friendly" as possible. The easiest approach would be to construct your manuals in the ISO 9000 format, that is, with the same section order and the same contents being addressed as the standard. Consider a multilevel approach to your manual as described for procedures. And remember that the more you write, the more they have to audit.

Two examples of the contents of a corporate-level manual are shown in Figure 5.3 and Figure 5.4. The first is "auditor friendly," and the second is less friendly and addresses the standard in a more indirect way. Both documents address the elements of the standard superbly. In the latter, outsiders (your potential customers as well as the auditors) will have a more difficult time finding how you cover each area. Why is this important? The American National Standards Institute (ANSI) has now made the ISO 9000 standard the national standard by which most current and future audits will be conducted. If you have a manual such as the less friendly one shown, consider creating a conversion index to help the auditors. This could be messy if you are splitting up multiple sections to address each ISO 9000 section, but it is better to plan in advance through the use of this conversion document than to wait until the auditors arrive for the documentation review.

At the second tier of your manuals, again try to stay within the constructs of the standard. Both the "auditor friendly" corporate-level manual and the second tier should be aligned to the standard. Starting with an effective manual is the first step in having a good audit, and more important, it demonstrates that you understand your business.

Training Records – We all live with the fear that some untrained rookie will come and repair our car's brakes, the plane's landing gear, or the control system of a nuclear power plant. The people who put our products together and take our orders need training (at Foxboro we do the nuclear power plants). ISO 9000 requires that training occurs and that it is reasonable for the given task. The proof the auditors are looking for is the training record that is maintained for every important task affecting the product. Certainly, you won't need a training record on how to open a door, but you will need records to show that the employees know how to operate the equipment associated with the product, that they have been trained on the assembly process, and, in all cases, how they can differentiate between good and bad workmanship. As you go through your procedure development, you will identify those tasks that affect the product, and from there you will be able to systematically identify the education and training needed for the job.

A generic training record developed by the ISO Steering Committee is shown in Figure 5.5. Prior to completing the training records, the supervisors would sit down with a group of employees performing the job and together identify what was required to perform the task. They would then create a checklist of the key attributes for which training

TABLE OF CONTENTS

Figure 5.3 An example of an "auditor friendly" table of contents from a corporate-level quality manual.

TABLE OF CONTENTS

Figure 5.4 An example of an "auditor unfriendly" table of contents from a corporate-level quality manual.

should occur and later confirm the employees' capability. At the end of this exercise, each employee performing this task will have a training record generated with the supervisor signed off on the employee's ability to perform the task prior to his or her being left alone on the job.

It is likely that as you are starting this ISO 9000 readiness activity, you do not have a training record for everyone who is performing jobs for which such a record would be appropriate. In this case, a retroactive

PERSONNEL TRAINING RECORD			
Name	Dept. #		
Title			
Education			
Formal Training			
Work Experience/On-the-Job Training			
Employee's Signature			
Supervisor's Signature			
Date			

Figure 5.5 A sample training record.

training record is acceptable, as long as you specify this is a one-time start-up policy. When Foxboro was audited, it was noted that there was quite a bit of "wet ink" on the documents. That was acceptable because the activities complied with the current procedures and the appropriate records were in place and demonstrated a "reasonable period of compliance." What is a reasonable period? If you can't decide, ask your auditor, as each situation is different.

Occasionally, a job will be defined as requiring a degree. You may have people in the job who do not have a degree. Make sure you have a procedure in place to allow capable nongraduates to comply with your requirements. Define a process for waiving the requirement and show the evaluation methods with a checklist.

Finally, the training records should be readily accessible to the supervisors, who are responsible for the record's accuracy and utilization. It is usually prudent to keep the records in the work areas and also possibly having the employees maintaining their own set. Some operations have determined that the records are to be maintained in the personnel files. If this is the case, consider two personnel files, as a number of employees consider it an invasion of privacy when an auditor or outsider goes through their personnel file.

When you let your employees maintain their own training records, you will discover they take an interest in them and will generally ensure they are accurate. The better employees will also seek additional training and want to keep growing—this is a win-win situation.

8 • *Educate All Employees On ISO 9000* – It takes a long time and repeated communications to get any message out to all corners of your organization. It is also essential that everyone comprehends the meaning and requirements of ISO 9000 as it requires the full participation of all employees. When you let everyone know why you are introducing an experience possibly perceived as painful, it will reduce the resistance to change and will gain support for continued compliance. This can be done by educating all employees through an employee newsletter, as seen in Figure 5.6, and involving the clear support of the senior member of the organization.

A Quality Improvement Newsletter for Employees of The Foxboro Company   January 1991

Total Quality is the Goal

Consistent with our pursuit of **total quality** at The Foxboro Company, we are in the process of becoming ISO 9001 certified. Achieving certification by late February will make Foxboro one of the first major US manufacturers to become certified across all its manufacturing facilities. Not only will this provide Foxboro with a competitive advantage, but it will also demonstrate to our customers that our business processes satisfy the requirements of the internationally accepted quality standard, ISO 9001.

Virtually every operation in the company is involved in the certification process and associated audits. Your management team strongly supports this activity and we appreciate the efforts of those directly involved in achieving this important goal.

S. S. Shaffran

ISO 9001: What is it?

ISO 9001 is one of the business quality standards which make up the ISO 9000 series. Certification demonstrates the capability of a supplier to control the processes that determine the acceptability of the product or service being supplied. The standards were

> **"As the international standard for quality systems, ISO 9000 serves to attest that the accredited supplier can demonstrate the ability to control the processes that determine the acceptability of the product."**

developed by the International Standards Organization (ISO), the international agency for standardization, headquartered in Geneva, Switzerland.

The International Standards Organization is composed of national standards bodies from 91 countries. The United States is represented in the ISO by the American National Standards Institute (ANSI). ANSI is composed of more than 250 US organizations and has historically determined the standards within the US. The American Society for Quality Control (ASQC) is a leading member of ANSI.

The ISO 9000 document is composed of a series quality standards that address different aspects of the business process. Firms will pursue certification for one of the standards listed below according to the their type of business.

ISO 9001- Confirms conformance to specified requirements during design, development, production, test installation and servicing.

ISO 9002- is used only when production, installation and servicing are needing conformance confirmation.

ISO 9003- is the least detailed

standard and requires conformance only in final test and inspection.

ISO 9004- contains guidance on technical, administrative and human factors affecting the quality of products and services. This standard is for internal use only and not to be used in contractual or certification situations.

ISO 9001 is a quality standard for the business process and not a certification for product reliability such as a "UL" approval.

What ISO 9001 Is Not

ISO 9001 is a generic standard and represents a minimum requirement for an effective quality system. By comparison, the Nuclear 10cfr50 and the Good Manufacturing Practices Criteria are more focused and require a higher level of commitment in certain areas. ISO 9000 does not tell you how to document your system, nor does it define what a Quality Manual is, or define what a quality plan is or what is an adequate Quality Policy.

Mr. Juran has pointed out that ISO 9000 provides no provision for continuous improvement, nor does it

Figure 5.6 Internal newsletter educates employees on ISO 9000.

When employees understand the requirements and why it is important to the company, they are less reluctant and do a better job. Through education, employees are mentally prepared for the very exhaustive preparation and audit. This preparation leads to confidence, which is apparent when they meet with the auditors.

Ongoing education also includes training your employees on how to deal with the auditors and how to respond to their questions. The education process extends over several months and requires multiple communications before the general population understands what ISO 9000 is all about. During this phase, continue to communicate the company's quality policy, as this will be part of the auditor's inquiry. You might also consider posting your quality policy every 60 meters and be confident that sooner or later the message will get through.

Keeping the management abreast of the organization's progress will also help the cause. By posting your progress measures, broken down by organization, you will ensure that those falling behind will receive the appropriate peer pressure (no senior manager wants their organization to be the reason for the company not being ready). About a month before the audit, you might want the supervision to hold group meetings across the company for final preparation and to answer final questions.

9 • Develop Operational ISO 9000 Management Teams – With the education of the ISO 9000 Steering Council and the preparation of all the documents and procedures, it becomes necessary to develop vehicles by which this information can be introduced into the organization and the momentum established to execute the various elements of the program. This can be accomplished by members of the ISO 9000 Steering Council setting up operational units within their own organizations, usually by department, educating them, and then going about installing the ISO 9000 elements that are relevant to that group. Figure 5.7 illustrates the how this was accomplished through the use of matrixed task teams at Foxboro.

The ISO 9000 Management Team members, once educated, act as the resident experts. When questions come up that they are unable to

Figure 5.7 Matrixed task teams assist in ISO 9000 audit preparation.

address, or do not feel comfortable with, the issues are brought to the ISO 9000 Steering Council. The ISO 9000 Steering Council develops a position or contacts the lead auditor of the certification agency for a disposition. The ISO 9000 Management Teams should consist of senior members of the various organizations with key supervisors from each group. Their primary tasks should encompass at least the following:

- Defining the flow within their organizations that will determine the areas affected by ISO 9000 (use flow charts). Reconcile duties at intersection points.
- Administer the progress measures.
- Assume responsibility for their area's conformance.

The compliance process should be managed on a weekly basis with the appropriate indicators in place to support visibility. In reality, this is when the project really gets its wings and develops a personality of its own. Encourage people to get involved and use the management-by-walking-around technique. There will be those who aggressively ask questions; answer them quickly. But don't assume that because some people aren't asking questions, all is well. In the beginning, they are most likely assimilating the changes and new requirements.

10 • Procedure Upgrades – Procedure upgrades will probably occur at all levels of the organization and in some cases this can involve an enormous amount of work. For most companies these procedures, more often then not, belong to the quality or industrial engineering departments, neither of which is staffed to support the load required to bring procedures up to compliance. While you may have procedures in place, in some areas they may be written one way whereas the job is performed in an entirely different manner — this is quite common.

If you have effectively deployed your operational ISO 9000 teams, they have identified the major informational flows and understand the documentation and record requirements. They have been able to identify where procedures are required. It's at this point that you should bring the real power of ISO 9000 to bear — the employees. The employees are the ones who know the actual task better than anyone else in your organization. Consider having them create the procedures. If you allow them to do this, you will enjoy the following pleasant benefits as we did at Foxboro:

• A potentially enormous work load is spread over a large group of employees rather than a few. This will ensure a shorter duration of the activity.
• The most qualified and most knowledgeable individuals will write the procedures ensuring that the practices align with the document.
• The employees will be made part of the process and feel like part of a team that is striving for the same common goal. You might even hear statements like "the company is finally starting to listen to us!"

Some in your organization may question the ability of their employees to write procedures, and in some areas they might be correct, but with a little help from their supervisors, most employees can draft a box and diamond flow chart. You can even write it up into a playscript format later, but that isn't necessary.

Once you have the draft procedure ready, have it reviewed by all the employees who perform the task. You might discover that they all don't agree. Treat this as an opportunity for a small group to go out and figure out the best of all worlds. We have a documented case where the yields in one of our areas showed a dramatic increase because of this exercise. Once the mini-team has come up with the best method, have all the employees sign the procedures. Not only will you have a training record that demonstrates the employee has been trained, you will also have a record of who else can perform the job in an employee's absence. You will also notice a higher sense of ownership among the employees and a willingness to follow the procedures. Should they have a suggestion and want a change, they know where to go to get it changed.

Any changes to the procedures should require a full review by all employees and a new set of signatures. This is effective for ensuring everyone participates in the change and prevents the "no one ever told me" response. Also you will quickly reveal any objections or problems to the change prior to installing the upgrade and driving the group into a state of instability.

Keep your quality and industrial engineers in on the process to make sure that the tasks and tools are proper and also that all the appropriate safety practices are invoked.

Procedures should be stored in the areas where they are used and where they are easily accessible to the employees performing the task.

Finally, the procedures should be the property of the local supervision and management. It needs to be made clear that maintaining structural process integrity is as much a part of the job as is building the product. The direct management should be responsible for controlling how their operations run, and it is their problem if they should cause the company to fail the basic business compliance test.

11 • *Establish Corrective Action Tracking* – One of the required elements of ISO 9000, Section 4.14, is the establishment of a corrective action process. Whereas the ISO 9000 series does not specifically state continuous improvement — and some would argue that this is the major shortfall of the standard — it does call for the establishment of a process that addresses methods used to prevent the reoccurrence of a problem and to employ an audit process that continually ensures that your operations meet the standard.

Historically, when an audit team swept through the areas attempting to verify compliance to the defined system, they would find nonconformities. A nonconformity would prompt the creation of a document noting the failure with the expectation that it would be resolved within a reasonable time frame. A problem occurs when the organization only addresses the individual item identified by the audit team. For example, in the past, if an audit uncovered an untrained employee, the response from the group would have been simply to go back and train that employee. The preferred response would be to determine the root cause for the employee not being trained, and to fix the process that allowed this finding to occur.

To remedy this undesirable type of response, at Foxboro we developed a document called a Quality Corrective Action Request (QCAR), as seen in Figure 5.8. The QCAR looks for the correction of the root cause of the problem, not the symptom. It requires identification of a

#1	THE FOXBORO COMPANY		DATE		C.Q.A. 3.17.2 Page 25
					QCAR #
#2	☐INTERNAL ☐EXTERNAL QUALITY CORRECTIVE ACTION REQUEST				
#3	TO:		RETURN TO: THE FOXBORO CO		
			ORIGINATOR'S NAME:		
			MAIL STOP:		
			ADDRESS		
#4	CLASSIFICATION OF DEFECT		NONCONFORMANCE REPORT #		
	☐CRITICAL ☐MAJOR ☐MINOR		ORDER #		
	REQUIRED RESPONSE (WORKING DAYS)		PART #		REF DOC
	☐___DAYS ☐15 DAYS ☐30 DAYS		LOT QTY		REJECTED QTY
	☐ IMPLEMENT NEXT ORDER		SUPPLIER TYPE #		
	PART OR ELEMENT NUMBER				
#5	PART OR ELEMENT DESCRIPTION				
#6	DESCRIPTION OF DISCREPANCY (INCLUDE DATA)				

THE FOLLOWING TO BE FILLED OUT BY THE PERSON ASSIGNED TO THE PROBLEM

#7	VERIFIED ROOT CAUSE
#8	CORRECTIVE ACTION PLAN
#9	CONTROLS TO PREVENT RECURRENCE ATTACH DATA/RESULTS DEMONSTRATING IMPROVEMENT.

10	COMPLETION DATE:		IMPLEMENTED NEXT ORDER #	
11	SIGNATURE	DEPT/COMPANY		DATE
12	ORIGINATOR'S VERIFICATION AND APPROVAL			
	APPROVAL YES ☐ NO ☐	VERIFIED BY :		DATE
13	REASON FOR NON APPROVAL:			

Figure 5.8 Quality Corrective Action Request (QCAR) addresses the root cause of a problem, not the symptom. Tracking QCAR status provides an indication of readiness for an ISO 9000 audit.

plan with a timetable for implementation and agreement between the initiator (auditor) and the operation that the root cause of the nonconformance will be corrected. Tracking the QCAR status by your audit teams provides the second key measure for the readiness of your organization. With QCAR visibility you will gain the confidence to move ahead with the ISO 9000 certification audit by third-party certification agents.

There is one drawback to the QCAR approach: It usually takes slightly longer to make the symptom go away. But the disease is cured and the patient thrives.

12 • Train Internal Audit Teams – Internal Audit is a requirement of the standard and provides you with visibility into the status of your operations. It is fairly common for a group of external corporate auditors to come by once a year and take a sample survey of the level of your organization's compliance and provide you with some form of a findings listing. This is a good approach for determining major problem areas, but it does not necessarily provide the organization with the refined visibility that you will need to successfully survive an ISO 9000 audit. As an analogy, suppose you come across a mouse in your kitchen. You call in the exterminator, a couple of traps are placed, and the next day a single mouse is caught. Did the exterminator confirm that you had a mouse? Yes. Were all the mice caught? Probably not. Remember the saying, "If you see a mouse, you have a dozen." There is a high probability that you will discover another mouse. Bringing in an exterminator on a one-shot basis just doesn't work. It is better to have a cat that is relatively inexpensive to maintain in return for its vigilance and hunting expertise. At Foxboro, a corporate team goes around annually and gives us a picture of the types of problems we might have. In addition, we also created a family of "cats," referred to as internal "mini-audit teams," as seen in Figure 5.9.

The primary purpose of the internal mini-audit team is to promote the self-auditing of an organization and to provide the visibility that an external organization lacks. We started with the premise that the employees who were involved in the work were most likely to know what

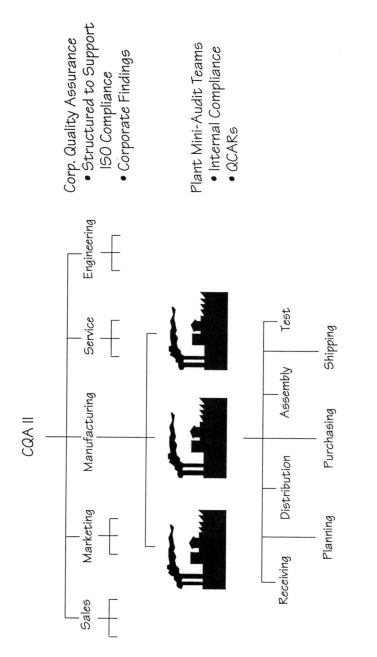

Figure 5.9 Mini-audit teams were used to promote the self-auditing of each organization and ensure readiness for the ISO 9000 audit.

was really happening in their own organizations and the ideal candidates to be on the internal mini-audit teams. We selected members from different parts of the organization and trained them on the requirements of ISO 9000 and how to conduct an audit. This training was actually developed and piloted in one of our plants, and then all the operations went through the training. An agenda of the program is provided in Figure 5.10. One trained auditor can certainly develop a course that will produce some very effective auditors.

At Foxboro, each operation established an audit team that systematically went through the respective organizations and conducted a thorough audit. In a typical plant, this team consisted of a buyer, a planner, an assembler, a warehouseman, and a certified lead auditor who was "home grown" and met American Society for Quality Control (ASQC) guidelines to form a complete plant mini-audit team. This team developed an aggressive schedule and went about auditing the organization. However, before the teams were sent out to do audits and generate QCARs, we recognized that we would need to change the mind-set of our management.

In the past, our management had developed an adverse sensitivity to audits and especially to findings. Yet we needed management to look at the findings (QCARs) in a very positive manner, for we intended this approach to work within their organizations.

We first convinced our senior managers that a QCAR issuance was in fact a positive event, and fortunately they had a positive response. They realized that as they were pushing their organization to move ahead quickly with scarce resources, some things would fall through the cracks. It's similar to a good basketball player — the better ones get four fouls in a game because they are playing aggressively while the ones who don't get any fouls either aren't being aggressive or they are on the bench. The senior managers took this position and reinforced it with their management teams.

This approach with the mini-audit teams had some very positive effects on the organization:

- Self-audit reduces the amount of anxiety within the operation. It had management support and was looked on as a method for improvement by the supervisors and employees.

PLANT AUDITOR TRAINING COURSE

THE FOXBORO COMPANY

PURPOSE

To train audit assist team members in the conduct required
to be involved with customer audits of The Foxboro Company
and to perform internal quality audits of a particular plant's
operations within the manufacturing division.

AGENDA

1	Become familiar with ISO 9001, 10CFR50, QCAR system, and audit checklist
2	Preaudit preparation
3	Preaudit interview
4	The audit
5	Postaudit conference
6	Final report
7	Follow-up, if required
8	Review of a previous customer audit of Foxboro
9	Perform a sample audit in a random area
10	Some do and don't rules
11	Findings vs. observations

LIMIT   Eight one-hour sessions

Figure 5.10 Plant auditor training course agenda.

- Having the existing staff perform the audits on a part-time basis reduced the need to fund additional staff.
- The employees looked upon this training as an opportunity for growth, as well as a return of control over their environment.
- The mini-audit teams were able to review the operations with their peers in a nondefensive manner, yielding a higher level of cooperation.
- This same audit team can also support a supplier survey program, applying ISO 9000 standards to suppliers. This also answered a common claim by suppliers that we might be holding them to a higher standard than our own organization. Your employees will also enjoy the opportunity to travel to a supplier's site, as it can generate some great ideas.
- There is also a unique phenomenon that is worthy of discussion. When the ISO 9000 auditors descend on your operations, you need to realize that they speak "ISOese" and probably don't understand your company terminology, nor do they understand your operations and systems. Each company "speaks" with a lot of home grown terms and acronyms. The ISO auditors will be asking questions in "ISOese" and the members of the mini-audit teams can be excellent translators. This is critical for ensuring that the proper messages are being communicated and reducing the actual stress among the groups, auditors, and the company. Mini-auditors can also help your employees feel more comfortable when approached by an auditor and can sometimes translate the questions into words the employee can understand. The mini-audit teams ensure that the auditors are being guided to the correct locations and that the responses fit the questions. Should an auditor receive an answer that seems incorrect, the issue can be dealt with before it escalates to a finding or observation. The mini-audit team member can also ensure that the auditors are receiving their answers quickly, as there is nothing more frustrating to an auditor than waiting for answers. During the audit at Foxboro, there were always two "audit assist members" from our audit teams with each ISO 9000 auditor. It was common for an ISO 9000

auditor to ask a question that would require one of the audit assist members to chase someone or something down, while the other remained to answer questions or escort the auditor. Most companies insist that visitors be escorted, and this includes auditors. You have an obligation to see they are not injured and that they are always taken to the correct locations.

• As stated earlier, mini-audit teams can provide tremendous visibility in assessing your readiness as well as projecting when you will be able to sustain a successful audit. In Foxboro's case, we tracked the number of QCARs generated by the mini-audit teams in the areas that indicated they were prepared for an audit. As noted, we considered the issuance of a QCAR as a positive indicator, and the retirement of a QCAR as another positive measure. We looked at open QCARs, those that had not yet been fixed, as less desirable, but also recognized that fixing a root cause of a problem often took time. Therefore, outstanding QCARs were considered more as an outstanding work load to be completed than as a problem. There was no pressure unless the organization had missed its own committed completion date. These measures were reported even to the president, who of course cheered on the management to generate QCARs.

More than 450 QCARs were initiated in the areas that claimed they were prepared for the audit (see Figure 5.11). The ISO 9000 audit occurred during February 1991, and we still had not closed all our QCARs. However, we did make sure they were minor and their fix status well documented. The ISO 9000 auditors, not surprisingly, found more on their own.

The deployment of the mini-audit teams in May 1990 with an aggressive schedule allowed us to determine our status by October 1990. We believed we would be ready in January of 1991, and thus arranged for a February 1991 audit. Establish an audit date that is reasonable, and hold to it. You will be amazed at how much you can accomplish when you and the organization can see them coming.

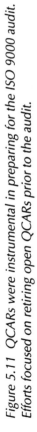

Figure 5.11 QCARs were instrumental in preparing for the ISO 9000 audit. Efforts focused on retiring open QCARs prior to the audit.

13 • *Use Corporate Audit Team to Verify Compliance* – The final step prior to the audit is to ensure that all the mini-audit teams have been effective. This can be determined by a Corporate Quality Assurance audit team, which not only must meet an annual audit requirement as typically defined in your own quality manual, but can use this as a vehicle for closing some remaining open findings. This team is highly visible and standalone. This group sweeps behind the plant mini-audit teams to verify that the teams are finding all the issues and that they are being corrected. Using the mini-audit teams and the corporate audit teams ensures a high degree of visibility and confidence. When the auditors first arrive, they may visit the corporate audit teams first and review the audits of the past year. This corporate-level group will meet the minimum requirement for ISO 9000. Again, the visibility of mini-audit teams is up to you. To push this "invisible mini-audit team" point a bit further, you may consider making the mini-audit teams exist only in an optional policy position format versus something required in your manual.

14 • *Certification Audit* – Now the fun begins. Your sales force has probably already promised the world that you will have certification and will most likely blame you for every order they lose until you become certified. The financial people have planned all those promised cost savings into next year's budget and now your president's career is tied in. You have continually reminded everyone that they don't want to be the ones that cause the company to fail — and you realize that goes for you too!

Where can it go wrong? The chart in Figure 5.12 supplied by the certification agents, Det Norske Veritas (DNV), provides some insight. DNV believes the root causes for findings are usually based on the following:

• Lack of understanding of the standard
• Lack of management commitment
• Lack of resources
• Customs of the trades

Figure 5.12 Percentage of system deficiencies registered against the requirements of ISO 9001. Source: Det Norske Veritas.

The certifying audit is extremely rigorous and comprehensive. Every site that was visited by DNV at Foxboro confirmed that "they don't miss anything, but they are fair."

In Foxboro's case, three auditors were on-site for three weeks going through three major manufacturing facilities and one very large design and administration complex. Generally, it would take three auditors four days to complete an audit of a facility and its associated support structure within the design and administration complexes.

A dedicated office area should be set aside for the auditors' use during their stay, and it should include copies of all the relevant documents they will require to get started. Copies of our corporate manual and each operation's corporate-level manual were kept there as well.

Treat the auditors as welcome guests, not as hostile, adversarial forces. Put yourself in their place: They are often away from home facing the discomforts of business travel like hotels, airports, long car rides, late planes, and rarely a good sound sleep. Usually, their interactions with people on the job are somewhat strained, given the nature of their work, and, when the job is done, they have a mountain of paperwork to do. This description might apply to many of us, in which case, you will understand all the more the importance of a gracious reception. See that they get good rooms on the quiet side of the hotel. If there is a suite, consider the expense as an investment toward having a more rested auditor visiting your site. A little consideration in these areas will be appreciated, especially if you are attempting to demonstrate and prove a critical position with an exhausted auditor. Attention to these details will add continuity to your self-portrayal as a company focused on quality at all times and levels.

Prior to the auditor's arrival, ensure that all the ISO 9000 Steering Council members know their roles and are ready to act as escorts between areas, along with your mini-auditors, if appropriate.

The Steering Council should consider meeting daily during the audit to review the previous day's results and implement plans to correct any findings prior to the conclusion of the audit. Depending on the type of agency you are using, it may be possible to correct a minor finding prior to the certification agent leaving the premises and thereby assist your meeting the minimum requirement or reduce the follow-up audit duration. It will also improve your score for those who operate under a scoring system.

Once the auditors are on site, bring them to your conference room and begin the orientation to the manuals as well as to the various safety and escort requirements. As stated earlier, promote a very open and friendly atmosphere. The auditors should have been selected with the understanding that they want you to succeed. On the other hand, they have their reputation to protect and the possibility of losing their certification is very real. Their job is to ensure that you have:

• Established a quality policy.
• Developed an appropriate quality system.
• Documented the system as required.
• Effectively implemented the system.
• Met the requirements of the ISO 9000 standard.

A typical audit goes proceeds in this manner: You greet the auditors, do the orientation, and assign team members. The lead auditor then takes control of the audit, and from then on the approach is at the discretion of this individual. The first stop might be a visit to your formal internal audit group where the auditors will ask to see the last year's internal audits. They want to confirm that you are actually conducting audits and will want to see schedules and activities associated with the audits, such as follow-ups to previous findings. They are also looking for trends, where your own audit teams repeatedly find problems. They will take their cues from the findings of these audits and look in the same areas. Finally, they are looking for open findings that are critical to the standard. If your own audit organization has left an open critical finding, it is an immediate "gotcha." If it is critical, the auditors will simply go to the area identified, confirm the shortfall, and thank you for inviting them as they head home. It is absolutely critical that all open corporate findings are closed.

After the auditors are firmly convinced that you have an aggressive audit program, they might make one more stop, prior to moving ahead with the audit in earnest. This next stop provided us with visible proof of the thoroughness of their audit and should also help you realize, as one of our employees so aptly stated, "you can't hide anything." They might visit your local accounting organization to gain access to all your departmental account codes, thereby ensuring access to all the desired areas and organizations. If you were thinking about making an organization disappear, or a tool room vanish, think again. Their methodology involved going to central information points first, then looking for abnormalities, and then making sure their audit plan incorporated an investigation of these abnormalities.

A typical example was that of Foxboro's calibration control. The audit team asked to see how calibration and the maintenance records were controlled. While they were verifying that the system existed, they also reviewed the records to see who had not returned tools. These locations then became the primary focus for investigation. With the team now armed with account codes and a year's worth of internal audit data they begin the process of investigation. This process usually follows the flow of the product, to your level of intended certification. In the case of ISO 9001, this means all the way back to your sales office.

You can expect that they will visit a local sales branch (if it is in your factory, that will be the logical target). They will ask where the orders come in, pick one up, and then say, "show me." The show me involves asking the employees how they handle the orders, how the orders are entered, and what do they do when they have a problem. The auditors may ask you to show them some training records (for both inside and outside employees; even the sales people if appropriate) and possibly ask questions like, "Do you have a quality policy? What is it?"

After the employees have come to grips with their nervousness, they point to the wall and say, "that's it" or mumble something about customer satisfaction and they begin answering the questions, and showing the necessary documents. When the auditors are satisfied, they will migrate down through your order scheduling department to again ask similar questions, with the focus on verifying that you are accurately processing the order and accurately quoting deliveries and handling the exceptions.

Finally, your order makes it to the production areas, and there the audit team will seem to split. The majority of the auditors' time, as much as 80%, will be spent in the manufacturing process. The rest of the audit team migrates up through engineering, design, and marketing.

As the audit team goes through engineering and design, the primary focus will be on two areas. A potential trouble spot can be the coordination of documentation between manufacturing and engineering. They will want to see not only that the proper documents are sent to manufacturing, but also that some form of acknowledgment is sent back to the originator ensuring that manufacturing has actually seen the documents. The other area is in the design review and sign off. The auditors will be looking to see a process that assures all the appropriate work has been completed to assure the product meets both the performance and safety requirements that it claims to support. They want a signature to verify that what has been designed is what marketing asked for and is what is being communicated to manufacturing.

The audit team will eventually migrate up to the marketing organization and verify the communication process between engineering and marketing. They will also look to ensure that what marketing is selling is in fact what engineering is being asked to design.

Meanwhile, the audit team on the assembly floor is interacting with your plant people. They will spend most of their time on the manufacturing floor and will generally avoid the supervision. They will walk into an area, introduce themselves, and ask what the employee does. After the employee describes his or her tasks to the auditors and it is relevant to the auditors' area of inquiry, the employee can expect additional questions such as:

- Do you have a quality policy here?
- Tell me about this machine; how do you operate it?
- Where are the procedures you consult if you have any questions? (The employee must be able to have easy access and personally show the auditors.)
- Were you trained before you started working alone, and could you get that record for me?
- How do you know when you are making the product correctly? Can you tell when it is good or bad? Show me. (Make sure there is some documented method for differentiation and that it was included as

part of the training record.)

- If you have a problem with the machine or material coming out, what do you do? (You will need a documented process outlined on how you control nonconforming materials.)
- How do you know those tools you are using are acceptable? Which ones need to be calibrated, and how do you know when to send them back?
- I noticed that you are using control charts. What do you do when they go out of control — like right there on the chart — what happened and what did you do? Could you show me the procedure and your training record on how you were trained on these charts? (Make sure your employees who are marking the charts are keeping records on those out-of-control events; the auditors are looking for some form of documented proof that the employee did take some action versus ignoring the event. Also ensure your charts are maintained in an on-line dynamic fashion. Charts updated after the product has left the area are in jeopardy of being considered ineffective to your preventative program.)
- How do you know you are building the right thing? Could you show me the assembly documents or model?

After the auditors have completed their questions they will apply a score or make a binary decision based upon the approach, the documentation, and the execution. The auditors will also look for documentation, old and current. Ensure that you have all your old documents (or models) removed or clearly marked, for example, "not for manufacturing use." They will be calling their fellow auditors who are visiting engineering and confirming revisions and dates. They will be looking at your test equipment to ensure not only that the equipment is under some form of calibration control, but also that the test requirements and outputs are those specified by engineering. They will look to see that your manufacturing operations have procedures for the update of these documents.

The auditors will progress through the operation to final testing, then to packaging, and on to shipping. They will also go into your service operations and will treat them as they would any manufacturing operation.

After finishing in the marketing and engineering areas, they will then descend upon your materials organization. They will review your planning operations — make sure you have a procedure on how you set master schedules. They will then focus on your purchasing, quality, and engineering interface. Your purchasing employees must be well versed in your supplier procurement process and the methods used to survey your suppliers and the materials being brought into your operation and the communications of changes with the supplier. After they are satisfied they will head out to your material handling areas. Ensure that your employees know their procedures and materials. For example, if you call for handling with Electro Static Discharge (ESD) bags, the employees need to be able to differentiate them from regular plastic bags and to be wearing a discharge device when they handle the materials. If a material is considered defective, ensure that it is maintained in a separate flow, and that all employees can recognize it as nonconforming material.

Upon completion of the materials areas the auditors will go to Incoming Inspection, looking for continuity between engineering and purchasing, as well as the usual competence and records.

After they have sufficiently covered all of the key points they will confer among themselves. You will probably already know the verdict, but they will officially tell you at the exit interview. If you pass, congratulations for achieving certification on the first audit. It is a major accomplishment.

If you fail the first time, you are in good company. Your challenge will be to salvage as much of the positive audit as possible and arrange with the auditors for a revisit, quickly. Each certification agent has his or her own approach, and it is best to clarify this early on and press the agents to live up to their earlier promises. If the audit goes badly initially, don't let them stop there — keep them going for two reasons. First, you need the visibility, and, second, your organization needs the exposure. You will pay more, but it will be worth it. If you will recall, you thought you were ready before the audit and without the auditors' visibility and their exposure to your management it is most likely you will have another bad experience, unless something changes. After two bad experiences you could be putting your career in jeopardy, as management will usually opt for a new team and coach.

Hopefully, you will have a positive audit and hold a celebration to congratulate the entire company as you all will have earned it. Eventually the certificate comes in and all is forgiven, but hopefully not forgotten. There is still the distinct possibility that when the auditors come back to close out some questionable findings, you could stumble, even though you had passed the first time. The other point is to realize that they will be back every six months (some auditors only every 12 months) to perform another shorter but more rigorous and in-depth audit focused on a specific operation. Passing these regular audits ensures continued ISO 9000 certification and causes you to get even better.

Also, remember, if one of your customers lodges a complaint against your operations, the auditor is likely to investigate the complaint at the next audit, or, if the complaint is serious enough, you may be required to move up the regularly scheduled audit.

6

What Do They Really Mean?

This chapter will go through the elements of the ISO 9000 standard as an auditor might. It will rephrase the ISO 9001 standard elements by section, in order to clarify and augment each area and to address the questions that would likely arise in reading the sections — at times you will read the standard and say, "what does it really mean?"

4.1 Management Responsibility

Deming, Juran, and other quality experts believed that management was primarily responsible for 80% to 90% of an organization's problems. Appropriately, management responsibility is the first element of the ISO 9000 standard.

4.1.1 Quality policy – Management must define and document its quality policy to ensure commitment to quality and to the minimum requirements of ISO 9000. Management must see that this policy is understood and implemented throughout the organization.

4.1.2 Organization – This subsection requires you to be able to prove that the template for your organization's quality approach is effective and defines responsibility. The standard calls for you to address problems systematically and solve them by attacking the root causes.

4.1.2.1 Responsibility and authority – An authority must be identified who can manage and verify that work affecting quality is performed as defined by your quality system. This person must have the freedom and authority to ensure the organization addresses nonconforming activities, maintains records of quality problems, and causes the organization to correct the nonconformities. This individual will later investigate and verify that the solution has succeeded. He or she must also be able to stop the operation or a shipment if required. Most companies provide an organization chart, with a path from the president down through the line personnel, with designated individuals having specific responsibilities for Quality Control or Quality Assurance.

4.1.2.2 Verification of resources and personnel – Management must maintain an in-house verification capacity for the primary purpose of conducting an internal audit. Audit personnel must be adequately trained for verification activities (see 4.18).

Internal auditors will be required to verify that your entire operation conforms to your quality plan, as well as to all the elements of ISO 9000. These audits need to be carried out on a regular basis (at least once per year) to ensure compliance. "Regular" means that your organization should be prepared to be audited by a third party at any given time with a high probability of passing.

The dynamics of your process and common industry practice will dictate the interval of your audits. Audits as described in this section must be carried out by a trained, independent party that is not immediately responsible for the area being audited.

These audits need to carry the appropriate level of documentation to satisfy the third-party auditors that they were carried out as part of an overall comprehensive plan for the audit of the organization and that they are rigorous in nature (i.e., you will be required to show comment and actions).

4.1.2.3 Management representative – A management representative must be designated to ensure that the requirements of ISO 9000 and all other defined quality standards are established and maintained.

People who are designated as the quality contacts can have multiple functions within your organization; therefore, it is not necessary that they have a strictly quality-related title. However, you need to be careful of the fox-in-the-hen-house syndrome. It is quite possible that your senior production manager within the manufacturing organization is responsible for total quality in his organization, including the verification and inspection aspects. If so, there needs to be a very strong case made, supported by documented evidence, that this individual is acting impartially and meeting the full intent of the standard. An easy way to define the quality responsibility is to designate quality responsibilities from the president to the assembly-line person on your corporate organization chart.

4.1.3 Management review – The management of your organization must regularly review the results of the quality system to determine that it is doing the intended job. This review should be based on measures that include the internal audit data and customer feedback, as well as appropriate incremental quality improvement data indicating the overall effectiveness of your system. You will need to document this review. These reviews should occur regularly or when an indicator reveals an undesirable result. If you have an active quality council, continually upgrading your operations, recordings of these meeting, and upgrades will effectively serve this requirement.

4.2 Quality System

You will need to document how you intend to meet the ISO 9000 requirements as well as the other standards that your customers require (e.g., who will be responsible for the execution of these programs and who will be responsible for the generation and maintenance of specific documents).

This section also requires that you document the needed tools, skills, resources, testing techniques, subjective features, design requirements, production processes, test procedures, and appropriate quality records and documents. Your higher-level manuals need to mention only these requirements. At the operating level, manuals must define and elaborate requirements relative to the particular area.

4.3 Contract Review

Your organization must have a systematic and documented method for ensuring that you understand and can meet your customers' needs. If your specifications differ from your customer requirements, there must be an orderly method for reconciliation. Finally, you must have a way to ensure that you have adequate capacity to meet the combined needs of all customers, if applicable. The ISO 9000 standard also suggests that ongoing communications be maintained with the customer during the life of the order as appropriate.

4.4 Design Control

4.4.1 General – This section requires you to maintain a documented process for the design of your product that produces the performance characteristics you promise your customers.

4.4.2 Design and development planning – This design plan must define how the design process will be carried out. It encompasses all levels of staff involved, their communications, and process paths. The design process must undergo regular and documented management reviews.

4.4.2.1 Activity assignment – Those in charge of design control must staff the function with appropriately trained people and equipment.

4.4.2.2 Organizational and technical interfaces – All interfaces between the design and other organizations required to design a product need to be identified. For example, marketing, sales, manufacturing, legal, and product safety. The information required for the design process from other organizations (input requirements) must also be defined.

4.4.3 *Design input* – You must have a defined system to ensure all appropriate design requirements are received by the design group. A listing of specifications and unique characteristics of the product must be maintained. The design group must actively communicate, detail, and resolve inconsistencies in the product requirements.

4.4.4 *Design output* – The output of the design process will include documented drawings, test requirements and tolerance requirements, materials specifications, appropriate assembly instructions, and test methodologies. Design output is to be documented and expressed in terms of requirements, calculations, and analyses. This output will also specifically reference all the appropriate regulatory or association standards and any critical requirements to the design that relate to the safe assembly and operation of the product.

4.4.5 *Design verification* – You will conduct a formal and documented review of the product design to ensure that all defined criteria are satisfied. This design review should include qualification testing and comparison with a similar design. As stated in section 4.1.2.2, this design review must be carried out by personnel independent of the design function (the supplier shall plan, establish, document, and assign functions for verifying the design to competent personnel).

4.4.6 *Design changes* – The process for making changes to your design should be documented. The routine should essentially meet the same criteria as those for a new design.

4.5 Document Control

4.5.1 *Document approval and issue* – All documents that are pertinent to the ISO 9000 standard must be under some type of formal documentation control, with procedures defining their establishment, review, upgrade, authorization, and removal upon obsolescence. These documents include your quality policy and objectives, quality manual, design controls, and records of work inspections, final inspections, instrument calibration, nonconformances, corrective actions, handling, storage and packaging, and internal audits.

The documents must be easily obtainable and usable. The organization that controls their usage must also ensure timely removal of documents or support some form of identification indicating they are no longer for use when revised documents are generated. Authorization of all procedures governing the documentation approval process requires formal approval.

4.5.2 Document changes/modifications – Any changes made to the documentation will require the same review and authorization that the establishment of the original document requires. When possible, an overview of the change to the document should be included with the new release. A full revision listing, table, or master list of currently active documents should be maintained and distributed to organizations that use them.

4.6 Purchasing

4.6.1 General–You are required to conduct your purchasing operations in a systematic fashion that ensures you are obtaining the proper materials for the organization's specified requirements.

4.6.2 Supplier (subcontractor) assessment – Assessment of a supplier must include a formal documented review methodology. The organization must maintain the assessment records of a supplier and a formal documented listing of suppliers who meet this approved process. This approved supplier listing must be available to those using it.

The supplier evaluation process used is based on the type of product being secured, past experience with the supplier, and its capabilities. In all cases, the assessment must specify the quality of the materials received.

Management must continually ensure that the controls are effective, with evidence of their review. Corrections to this process should include procedural updates.

> *Note of clarification: ISO 9000 certification of your supplier is not an enforced element, nor does it specifically require that your supplier become certified or even compliant with the ISO 9000 standard at this time.   If a third-party certification agent requires supplier certification as a condition for representing your products as coming from an ISO 9000 certified process, it is a discretionary policy invoked solely by the third-party certification agent.   The issue of compliance is addressed in section 4.6.3, and that requirement is at your discretion.*

4.6.3 *Purchasing data* – The material being purchased must be fully described. This includes specific part identification. You will also describe process requirements, inspection instructions, special markings, and any other detailed information relevant to the acceptance of the material.

The purchase document must include notation of compliance to any relevant standard (ISO 9000 may be one of those standards). Prior to the release of the specification requirement to the supplier, an appropriately trained individual must review it to ensure adequacy. This individual can be the originator of the requirement.

4.6.4 *Verification of purchased product* – It is the purchaser's option to perform a source inspection of the product or to perform the inspection on the purchaser's site. In either case, inspection location does not absolve the supplier of the responsibility to inspect and fully comply with its own quality policy, as described to the purchaser. If the purchaser provides for source inspection at the supplier's site, the purchaser does not surrender the right to reject the material at any later time.

4.7 Purchaser Supplied Product

You must establish procedures for the storage, handling, and maintenance of materials provided to you by your customer for eventual incorporation into a supplied product. Should this material become unusable for any reason, it must be segregated, identified, and reported to your customer.

This could be considered a "mirror" policy of your expectations and policies for the proper handling of your own materials. Your supplier's unique expectations will be defined in the initial contract, and procedures will be required to support such activities.

4.8 Product Identification and Traceability

You must maintain procedures for the proper identification and documentation of materials as they move through the production, installation, and delivery processes to ensure that the customer's requirements are satisfied.

Second, depending on your customer's requirements, you may need to address production lot identification or component traceability. The standard says this is to be done "where appropriate," meaning as required by your customer. Your customer may request that your product have varying degrees of traceability. It is your responsibility to ensure there are formal and documented methods in place to demonstrate compliance with your customer's requirements.

4.9 Process Control

Process control refers to the entire process of producing a product and the method by which you control and ensure that your processes are followed — it is not limited to some form of statistical process control. The standard frequently uses the term "procedures" when referring to process control.

4.9.1 General – You must provide a controlled work environment that ensures that the quality of the product is adequate and in conformance with the documentation and record requirements of ISO 9000. This requires you to provide adequate and controlled written instructions or representative samples that ensure proper assembly and workmanship standards. These standards should define the criteria for acceptable workmanship.

The process should define the equipment, environment, reference standards, and quality plans, and must include regular monitoring during production. The equipment used by the employees must have appropriate operating instructions and maintenance plans.

Work instructions must be reviewed by authorized personnel. These instructions are required whenever their absence could adversely affect the quality of the output. The instructions should be reviewed periodically to ensure adequacy and proper alignment with other procedures.

4.9.2 Special processes – A "special process" is any process that cannot be fully confirmed through testing or inspection so that a defect only surfaces when the product is being used by the customer. Typical examples are welding, paint applications (Zyglow inspection), and heat treatment of materials. These processes require identification as special processes, operation by appropriately trained personnel using qualified equipment, and continuous monitoring with supporting records. Special processes must also meet the full requirements of section 4.9.1 (general process control).

4.10 Inspection and Testing

This section deals with the testing of materials and products as they move through the process. As a minimum, you must always have requirements that clearly specify tolerances or ranges. You must also have a defined and documented process for the handling of nonconformance. This requires some form of segregation and identification.

4.10.1 Receiving inspection and testing – No material should be incorporated into the product without verification to the product specifications. If, due to emergency, the incoming material is used without verification, it will require designated authorization, full documentation, and tracking. All preverified materials should be maintained in a segregated area according to a documented process.

The verification of the incoming product must conform to your quality plan and documented procedures. Verification can take many acceptable forms and is not necessarily delegated to the receiving inspection organization.

4.10.2 In-process inspection and testing – You must document your in-process inspection procedure and carry out the defined inspections. The level of in-process inspection is determined by your own operations, and, with the exception of special process inspections, there is no additional requirement.

If in-process inspection is required, you will need to provide holding points for nonconforming materials. The ISO 9000 standard encourages the use of in-process inspection as a method for minimizing defects and allows in-process inspections to act as part of the final inspection and test if appropriate.

4.10.3 Final inspection and testing – You are required to perform a full inspection and test of your final product as specified in your quality plan and documented procedures. This full inspection and test must verify that the inspection data fully meet the specifications of the product, as defined by your quality plan. Final inspection should incorporate the results of previous inspections and their successful satisfaction of requirements. You are required to hold the product and defer its shipment or release until all inspections have been completed and the product has met all the specifications.

4.10.4 Inspection and test records – You must keep records to demonstrate that your product has met the testing requirements and that all the tests were conducted per your quality plan (also see section 4.16).

4.11 Inspection, Measuring, and Test Equipment

You must ensure the proper maintenance and control of *all* of your final test, calibration, and any other test equipment (including jigs, fixtures, templates, patterns, and software) as defined by your quality plan. This equipment must be capable of measuring to the level of accuracy specified in the test requirements. Your employees must have been training in the use and proper applications of the equipment. If your customers request the design verification data so as to conduct their own study to determine functional adequacy, they must be made available to them. To comply with this section of the standard, you should:

a. Identify what measure is to be made, by what piece of equipment, to what specific tolerances.
b. Calibrate the equipment at regular intervals of time or usage. The calibration of this equipment must be compared with a known "good" with a clear path to a nationally recognized standard. Calibration cycle times are usually based on the manufacturer's guidelines, or less often by history and usage.
c. Have a calibration system to identify the equipment to be controlled, where it is used, the method for confirmation, the frequency of inspection, and procedure for when it is out of conformance.
d. Ensure that the equipment is capable of meeting the requirements and document it.
e. Place some type of identification mark on the equipment to show its current calibration status.
f. Maintain records on the calibration.
g. Document the occurrence and return to the prior calibration for review should you find a device out of calibration. When a nonconformance trend is indicated, correct the nonconformance by shortening the calibration cycle or replacing a tool.
h. Ensure that the area is suitable for the testing and usage of the equipment.
i. Properly store and maintain (through employee training) the calibration equipment.

j. Permit only authorized personnel to make adjustments to the equipment or software.

Not all your measurement or calibration equipment is required to satisfy the previous requirements, only those used in the final product test inspections or as defined in your quality plan. If in-process inspections are used to validate requirements within the process, and they support your final inspection and testing activity, then they must be made part of your calibration control scheme. Should you determine that a particular instrument is not required to meet the ISO 9000 criteria, then you may exempt it by identifying it as such. However, keeping as many pieces of equipment as possible in compliance with these requirements will help you to produce the best product at the lowest cost and achieve the goal of zero defects. Third-party certification agents take a dim view if you try to stipulate that only your final test equipment needs calibration control. They will usually cite a failure in your corrective action process if you attempt to use this loophole. We advise that you discuss this with your auditor beforehand.

4.12 Inspection and Test

As products go through the various testing areas, the material and products must carry identification relative to their status. Identification can include stamps, labels, tags, records, or diskettes. Those products that fail to meet the testing or inspection criteria should be physically separated from the rest. This identification should follow the product through the entire production process. These records must indicate the authorized person who allowed the proper release of the product. These records shall conform to section 4.16, quality records requirements.

4.13 Control of Nonconforming Product

Upon identification of a nonconforming material or product, the item must be segregated and identified as such. All operations must have procedures in place to define the process that handles the nonconformance. When appropriate, the nonconformance must carry documentation that will support the evaluation of the product and disposition. A notification of the nonconformance and disposition shall be forwarded to all parties affected or involved in the nonconformance.

4.13.1 Nonconformance review and disposition – The evaluation of nonconforming material must be conducted by an authorized individual as defined by your documented procedures. If the authorized individual determines that the product is acceptable as is, or requires a regrade, a return, or is to be scrapped, the accompanying document will reflect this activity and only then may you proceed to process the material. Should the authorized agent determine that rework or repair is required, the original document outlining the nonconformance must remain active until a reinspection of the material is done and only then may the issue be closed. The document prepared for the identification of the nonconforming product should include a description of the inadequacy, and a full description of the activities required for correction and disposition.

4.14 Corrective Action

You are required to take corrective actions based on any customer complaint, service failures, audits of operations, and quality records. This action must look for the root cause of the problem and put corrective procedures and practices in place that will prevent future occurrences. Your organization must put controls in place to ensure that all corrective actions are carried out and that they have been effective.

4.15 Handling, Storage, Packaging, and Delivery

4.15.1 General – All activities related to the handling, storage, packaging, and delivery of the product must have fully documented and maintained procedures.

4.15.2 Handling—Your methods for handling must ensure the product remains undamaged and will not suffer from deterioration. This includes full documentation of methods and training to ensure safety of personnel and product.

4.15.3 Storage—You must have secure and segregated storage of raw and finished materials to prevent deterioration, damage, and mixing. You must also have documented methods for the transfer of the materials. Documented procedures and methods should also include the regular assessment of the stored materials to ensure material integrity.

4.15.4 Packaging – The operation must maintain formal and documented packaging procedures, marking requirements, and instructions. The packaging instructions must be documented, preservation methods outlined, and equipment used that will not damage the materials. Personnel must be trained in the packaging techniques and equipment used. The product should be marked in accordance with specifications. The materials must remain segregated and maintained until the product has been accepted by the customer, or per contract agreement.

4.15.5 Delivery – Delivery of the product is made in accordance with the customer contract. Special protection should be extended to support the intact arrival if specified. The delivery methods and practices must be documented and the employees trained for this task.

4.16 Quality Records

You must retain records that verify product compliance to requirements. Your records must also demonstrate the verified effectiveness of your operations through internal audits, corrective actions, senior management reviews, assessment of suppliers, calibration, training, customer contracts, design reviews, product nonconformances, inspection and testing, and product identification.

Records should be defined, filed, and maintained to allow for easy access. They should identify the process and products involved. Record retention procedures must be documented and support customer agreements. Quality records must be stored for minimum deterioration, easy retrieval, and for a reasonable period of time (e.g. warranty period).

4.17 Internal Quality Audits

You must carry out a comprehensive review of your organization to verify the effectiveness of your quality system and compliance with the ISO 9000 standard. This review should take the form of scheduled audits of the various areas, based on the relative importance of the operations and activities. Audits are to be conducted in accordance with your documented procedures by trained individuals. The results of the audits must be documented and presented to management personnel for timely corrective action of any nonconformances cited, and tracked to ensure follow-through.

Audit frequency will be determined based on experience as well as the importance to the products being produced. Generally, no more than one year should elapse between audits of the same area to maintain compliance.

Audits are carried out according to a documented plan that will specify not only locations and time, but also the qualifications of the auditors, the output required, the method for conducting the audit, and who will receive the results. Audits shall be conducted by personnel independent of the operation being audited and trained in ISO 9000 requirements.

4.18 Training

Training must be provided and documented for personnel whose activities affect product quality. Personnel must be trained in the specific tasks assigned, qualified to perform these tasks, and supported with documentation and records of training. These records must be maintained to reflect the current task.

Your quality plan must outline the procedures for identifying the tasks that require training. Training can be based on formal education, supervised training on the job, or past experience. In any case, a formal record must be maintained and approved by an authorized individual as defined by in the procedures.

4.19 Servicing

Based on your policies and customer contracts, you will provide service to the level defined in your quality plan. All those activities performed must comply with the ISO 9000 standard. You will develop plans, procedures, training, documentation, and testing methods to support the committed level of service .

4.20 Statistical Techniques

You may use statistical techniques to validate the product, material, or process. These techniques must be documented and approved. Operators must be trained and demonstrate proficiency.

The ISO 9000 standard is interpretive to accommodate different types of businesses. It is important to ensure that your interpretation is shared by your auditor. Consider the rephrasing of the standard in this chapter as a supplement to other guidance documents such as ISO 9004.

Appendix 1

Are You Ready?

The following questions will help you gauge your readiness. They are organized for specific organizations within the firm including:

- Management
- Order Processing
- Research, Design, and Development
- Planning
- Procurement
- Stores/Material Handling
- Production
- Inspection
- Shipping/Transport
- Servicing

Consider asking your major organizational groups to verify that they can answer each of the questions under their heading. These questions could also become the basis for review by your internal audit organizations. Although they are not all inclusive, be assured that if you don't ask them, the ISO 9000 auditors will.

Management

4.1 Management Responsibility
☐ Have you documented your quality policy and stated your corporate mission clearly?
☐ Is there an ISO 9000 program manager?

☐ Is your organization trained to understand your quality policy, and is the policy being maintained?

☐ Are there job descriptions that define quality authority and responsibility?

☐ Are trained individuals assigned to internal audit activities and are their audit reports transmitted to senior management?

☐ Has management reviewed all final inspection and test procedures to ensure adequacy and compliance with customer contracts?

☐ Is the total quality system reviewed by management regularly?

☐ Is there a senior management representative with the responsibility and authority to ensure effective problem resolutions according to the procedures?

☐ Is there a sufficient number of trained people allocated for verification?

☐ How does management adequately ensure ISO 9000 compliance?

4.3 Contract Review
☐ Does management review your ability to meet contractual commitments?

4.4 Design Control
☐ Are design activities formalized and cohesive?

4.5 Document Control
☐ Is the documentation system reviewed and approved by management?

4.13 Control of Nonconforming Product
☐ Is disposition authority defined?

4.14 Corrective Action
☐ Has management reviewed the process for corrective action and verified that all requirements are met?

☐ How has management demonstrated involvement in the corrective action process?

4.16 Quality Records

☐ Do you have records of management review of the quality system?

4.17 Internal Quality Audits

☐ Do you have records of management review of internal audits, schedules, and results?

4.18 Training

☐ Has management ensured that the training program requirements have been documented and implemented?

Order Processing

4.1 Management Responsibility

☐ Has responsibility for contract review been defined?
☐ Have contract review activities been defined?

4.3 Contract Review

☐ Are there procedures established to support customer inquiries?
☐ Are order preparation and review procedures established to ensure that customer requirements can be met?
☐ Are methods established for clarifying customer orders when they are incomplete or unclear?
☐ How do you verify proper translation of customer orders into internal work orders?
☐ Are communications to customers clearly defined and formalized?

4.5 Document Control

☐ Are there clear procedures for the creation of internal work orders based on customer contracts?

☐ Are customer change order procedures documented and properly processed?

☐ Are methods in place to communicate changes in product status to customers with existing contracts?

4.13 Control of Nonconforming Product

☐ Are customer complaints documented and supported by written procedures and their disposition monitored?

4.14 Corrective Action

☐ Is there an effective corrective action process employed to eliminate ongoing customer complaints, and is it reviewed to ensure root cause problems are remedied?

4.16 Quality Records

☐ Are records of customer contracts properly maintained for the required period?

☐ Are customer complaints recorded and maintained for analysis?

4.17 Internal Quality Audits

☐ Have corrective actions been initiated based on deficiencies found during internal audits?

4.18 Training

☐ Has the sales staff been trained and are records available?

Research, Design, Development

4.1 Management Responsibility

☐ Are the quality policy and objectives documented in the design organization?

☐ Is your organization trained and does it understand your quality policy?

☐ Are there job descriptions that define authority and responsibility within the group and at each level of review?

☐ Are designs systematically verified against specifications by parties independent of those doing the actual work?

4.2 Quality System

☐ Are there documented procedures and defined processes for the development of a design?

☐ Are your design input and output requirements defined?

☐ Do design output requirements incorporate regulatory requirements as well as crucial safety requirements?

☐ Do you have procedures for formal design review?

☐ What are your procedures for design changes?

4.3 Contract Review

☐ Do you have contract review procedures for specific customer designs?

4.4 Design Control

☐ Are organizational interfaces specific to a contract defined and are the appropriate employees aware?

☐ Are requirements available to production for inquiry?

☐ Are inputs to the design process and outputs (work leaving the design process to another group or customer) reviewed for adequacy and verified to meet customer and regulatory requirements?

☐ Has design review incorporated alternate calculations and comparisons to similar designs?

☐ Do output documents adequately define material and methods requirements?

4.5 Document Control

☐ Are revisions handled to properly control changes to documents, codes, software, and standards?

☐ Are handwritten revisions dated and signed by an authorized individual and reissued within a reasonable period of time?

☐ Are there methods for the recall of a design document?

4.6 Purchasing

☐ Are interfaces with procurement defined and specifications reviewed to ensure receipt of proper information?

4.8 Product Identification and Traceability

☐ Does your documentation provide for clear identification of the product and materials as well as traceability?

4.9 Process Control

☐ Does documentation provide for adequate workmanship, methods, and material acceptance instructions?

☐ Do work instructions contain adequate equipment, consumable, and environmental information?

4.10 Inspection and Testing

☐ Do adequate procurement, inspection, test instructions, documents, and records exist to ensure acquisition of required goods?

4.11 Inspection, Measuring, and Test Equipment

☐ Do documented calibration procedures exist that require the identification and location of equipment?

☐ Are methods defined for calibration and revision of all equipment and software.

4.16 Quality Records

☐ Are design review records maintained, retrievable, and storage adequate?

4.18 Training

☐ Are training requirements reviewed regularly for adequacy?

4.20 Statistical Techniques

☐ Are the procedures for the application of statistical tools adequate and reviewed for effectiveness?

Planning

4.1 Management Responsibility

☐ Are your quality policy and objectives documented?

☐ Is your organization trained and does it understand your quality policy?

☐ Are there job descriptions that define authority and responsibility?

☐ Is capacity verified against contract requirements for adequacy?

☐ Are work orders and instructions verified against customer contract by those not doing the work?

4.2 Quality System

☐ Are master scheduling and work order procedures established and documented?

4.4 Design Control

☐ Are interfaces with design, production, and shipping formalized?

4.5 Document Control

☐ Are procedures established for control and distribution and changing of documents?

☐ Does revision status align with documents maintained in engineering and documentation control?

☐ Are obsolete documents and schedules promptly removed?

☐ Are approved work orders released per procedures?

4.6 Purchasing

☐ Is the interface with procurement, sales, and production documented?

☐ Are communications with subcontractors formalized to incorporate methods, specifications, and inspection, testing, and personnel qualifications?

☐ Are requisitions for subcontractors reviewed by authorized individuals for compliance to specifications?

4.7 Purchaser Supplied Product

☐ Does the purchaser notify your organization of supply problems with materials in a formal manner? Is there a documented process for updating your planning?

☐ Are records maintained for evaluation of purchaser supplied product?

4.9 Process Control

☐ Are production schedules and activities executed according to procedures?

☐ Do work instructions include descriptions, parameters, sequences, tooling requirements, reporting, and special skills requirements?

4.10 Inspection and Testing

☐ Are the interfaces with inspection and testing and specific hold points defined as part of your planning?

4.11 Inspection, Measuring, and Test Equipment

☐ Is the availability of inspection and testing equipment considered in your plan?

4.16 Quality Records

☐ Are planning records maintained and easily retrievable per your documented plans and requirements?

4.18 Training

☐ Are your training requirements established and regularly reviewed?

4.20 Statistical Techniques

☐ Are the procedures for the application of statistical tools reviewed for effectiveness?

Procurement

4.1 Management Responsibility
☐ Does your organization understand your quality policy?
☐ Are there job descriptions that define authority and responsibility for ensuring the proper assessment of suppliers?

4.2 Quality System
☐ Are there established procedures for subcontractor assessment and are they followed?
☐ Do these procedures incorporate inquiries and methods for source as well as receiving inspections?

4.4 Design Control
☐ Is the information stream between procurement and design documented?

4.5 Document Control
☐ Are procedures for the distribution of documents, change orders, and purchase order reviews established and employees trained in their use?
☐ Is a current listing of approved suppliers available?
☐ Do drawing revisions sent to suppliers align with those in planning and engineering?
☐ Are purchase orders and changes reviewed and approved prior to being released?

4.6 Purchasing
☐ Are subcontractors selected based on records of performance?
☐ Do you have a supplier rating system and a maintained listing of authorized/approved suppliers?
☐ Do the procedures define the handling of source inspections as well as the relationships between types of purchased products and inspection methods?

4.16 Quality Records

☐ Are the performance and nonconformance records of the suppliers adequately maintained and reviewed?

☐ Are records of supplier audits maintained?

4.18 Training

☐ Are procurement function training records available and reviewed regularly?

☐ Is the staff competent to perform the assigned tasks?

4.20 Statistical Techniques

☐ Are sampling procedures established for suppliers that ensure product conformity?

☐ Are sample sizes taken to plan and are records used to determine the relationship with the supplier and the inspection methods used?

Stores/Materials Handling

4.1 Management Responsibility

☐ Are there job descriptions that define quality authority and responsibility?

4.2 Quality System

☐ Are monitoring and maintenance of materials procedures defined and documented?

4.5 Document Control

☐ Are procedures established for the issuance of work orders and materials disbursement and for changes to these instructions?

☐ Are out-of-revision documents removed from the area?

4.6 Purchasing

☐ Are communications with purchasing formalized?

☐ Is the movement of materials to and from stores formalized, documented, and authorized?

4.9 Process Control

☐ Is the amount and type of materials receiving inspection clearly defined by product or type?

☐ Are the procedures established for reinspection of aged materials and are records maintained?

☐ If materials don't conform, are they separated from the normal flow and identified as nonconforming per your documented procedures?

☐ Are performing operators receiving inspections according to defined procedures?

4.12 Inspection and Test Status

☐ Are there methods and documents for indicating that a product or material has been satisfactorily inspected and released by the appropriate authority?

4.13 Control of Nonconforming Product

☐ Are there procedures for the handling and disposition of nonconforming products and materials?

☐ Do these procedures include responsibility for review and authorization for release?

☐ Do nonconforming products and materials that require corrective action remain identified as nonconforming until passing reinspection?

4.14 Corrective Action

☐ Are documented investigative procedures in place to determine the cause of nonconforming materials?

☐ Are records of these investigations kept and have these been used for the evaluation of suppliers?

4.15 Handling, Storage, Packaging, and Delivery

- ☐ Do the documented procedures include location and storage tracking, identification, handling of open packaging, handling nonconformities, FIFO inventory cycling, and storage environments?
- ☐ Do the methods ensure adequate environmental protection and size?
- ☐ Are products identified and materials handled according to shelf-life requirements?

4.16 Quality Records

- ☐ Are records of supplier performance, inspection, samples, nonconformance disposition, and subcontractor quality maintained per procedures and requirements?

4.20 Statistical Techniques

- ☐ Are sampling procedures established for materials that ensure product conformity?
- ☐ Are sample sizes taken to plan and are records used to determine the relationship between the materials and the inspection method used to validate effectiveness?

Production

4.1 Management Responsibility

- ☐ Is your organization trained to perform the production activity and does it understand your quality policy?
- ☐ Are there job descriptions that define quality authority and responsibility?
- ☐ Have you assigned and trained a person to monitor your process and product?

4.2 Quality System

- ☐ Are monitoring procedures for your process and products documented with acceptance characteristics and criteria?

☐ Are procedures for test and inspection documented?

4.4 Design Control
☐ Are design interfaces defined and documented?

4.5 Document Control
☐ Are there procedures for the distribution and removal of documents, and are all obsolete documents removed?

4.6 Purchasing
☐ Is the removal of materials from stores by production coordinated with planning and are these methods documented in formal procedures?

4.8 Product Identification and Traceability
☐ Can operators identify all materials and products and ensure traceability throughout the entire process as defined by your procedures?

4.9 Process Control
☐ Are production schedules available?
☐ Are monitoring procedures established and results documented?
☐ Is there a documented method for determining a special process and have those areas been defined?
☐ Have operators been trained and qualified to operate process equipment and has the equipment been reviewed and approved for effectiveness?
☐ Are the environment and equipment suitable for the production tasks?

4.10 Inspection and Testing
☐ Is the relationship between inspection and monitoring clearly defined to include intervals, amount, and frequency?
☐ Are all products inspected prior to release, and are nonconforming products held or separated from the process?

☐ Are nonconforming products clearly identified and remain so until a plan of action is completed and the material undergoes a full reinspection?

4.11 Inspection, Measuring, and Test Equipment

☐ Do the inspection and test criteria also include the equipment and software to be used?

☐ Does the test equipment have a calibration indicator of the current status?

☐ Are these tools and indicators safeguarded from unauthorized adjustments?

4.12 Inspection and Test Status

☐ Do inspection procedures require the identification of test status by marking, location, or supporting documents?

☐ Is there a formally designated individual/group responsible for determination and action related to nonconforming products or materials?

4.13 Control of Nonconforming Product

☐ Are there procedures for the handling and disposition of nonconforming products?

☐ Do these procedures include responsibility for review and authorization for release?

☐ Do nonconforming products that require corrective action remain identified as nonconforming until reinspection is complete?

4.14 Corrective Action

☐ Do you have documented procedures that call for the investigation of nonconforming products or materials?

☐ Can you demonstrate how your corrective action process has resulted in the changing of your processes and procedures and how it has been effective in preventing nonconformances?

4.15 Handling, Storage, Packaging, and Delivery

☐ Are there formal procedures established for the effective preservation and protection of materials used in production?

☐ Are these materials preserved and dispatched according to these procedures?

4.16 Quality Records

☐ Are monitoring, inspection, test, sample, process equipment, personnel, process analysis, production activities, and nonconformance records maintained as required by your quality policy and customer contracts?

☐ Are these records easy to retrieve?

4.18 Training

☐ Are production employee training records reviewed regularly to ensure adequacy and conformance?

☐ Are those employees who are involved in special processes fully qualified with supporting training documents?

☐ Do all your employees comply with the background or education requirements as you have defined in your training requirements?

4.20 Statistical Techniques

☐ Are sampling procedures established for materials that adequately ensure product conformance?

☐ Are procedures established to verify that the process being used is in control?

Inspection

4.1 Management Responsibility

☐ Are there functional job descriptions that define quality authority and responsibility?

☐ Is there a formal organization established for in-house audits that is adequately staffed and trained?

4.3 Contract Review

☐ Are contract review procedures established that ensure the availability of information and the validation of the contract?

☐ Are records retained to support the contract review activity?

4.4 Design Control

☐ Are design interfaces defined and documented?

4.5 Document Control

☐ Are your procedures reviewed and authorized by the appropriate personnel?

☐ Do you have documentation control procedures that ensure the availability of current documents at the appropriate locations and the removal of obsolete revision documents?

☐ Are changes approved by an authorized individual and identified through a revision document?

4.8 Product Identification and Traceability

☐ Are there procedures for identification of the material/product through the entire production process?

4.9 Process Control

☐ Are procedures/work instructions available in areas where quality depends on them?

☐ Are these procedures/work instructions being followed?

☐ Are special processes identified and are there methods in place to ensure that they are being reviewed?

4.10 Inspection and Testing

☐ Are procedures in place for effective incoming material inspection and documentation?

☐ Are materials held until they are identified as acceptable for production?

☐ Do you have defined procedures for allowing nonverified materials into production with the proper authorization identified?

☐ Are nonconforming products segregated from the flow and positively identified?

☐ Are there procedures for verification of materials during inspection?

☐ Are all appropriate inspection documents completed prior to the material being released?

☐ Are all inspection records and documents properly maintained?

4.11 Inspection, Measuring, and Test Equipment

☐ Do the inspection and test criteria include the equipment and software to be used, and are these appropriate for the task defined?

☐ When performing inspection, are the appropriate materials and equipment available, and are they maintained to the correct precision as defined by your calibration program?

☐ Does the test equipment have an indicator of the current calibration status?

☐ Are these tools and indicators safeguarded from unauthorized adjustments?

☐ Do you perform a reinspection when your testing equipment is found to be out of calibration or malfunctioning?

☐ Can you produce records to prove the reinspection?

☐ Are methods established for the proper care and storage of test equipment and software?

☐ Are regular checks performed on the test equipment and software to verify conformance?

4.12 Inspection and Test Status

☐ Do inspection procedures require the identification of test status by marking, locating, or supporting documents?

☐ Is there a formally designated individual/group responsible for determining nonconforming products or materials?

4.13 Control of Nonconforming Product
- ☐ Are there procedures for the handling and disposition of nonconforming products?
- ☐ Do these procedures include responsibility for review and authorization for release?
- ☐ Do all nonconforming products that require corrective action remain identified as nonconforming until reinspection is complete?

4.14 Corrective Action
- ☐ Do you have documented procedures that call for the investigation of nonconforming products or materials?
- ☐ Can you demonstrate how your corrective action process has changed inspection processes and procedures and has been effective in preventing nonconformances?

4.16 Quality Records
- ☐ Are monitoring, inspection, test, sample, and nonconformance records maintained as required by your quality policy and customer contracts?

4.18 Training
- ☐ Are those employees who are involved in inspection processes fully qualified with supporting training documents?

4.20 Statistical Techniques
- ☐ Do you have procedures for identifying acceptable statistical methods to be employed for inspection?

Shipping/Transport

4.1 Management Responsibility
- ☐ Are your quality policy and objectives documented?

☐ Is the organization trained?

☐ Does it understand your quality policy?

☐ Are there job descriptions that define authority and responsibility for verifying the quality of the shipping/transport work being performed?

☐ Are requirements for the verification of shipment accuracy available in the area?

4.3 Contract Review

☐ Are contract requirements for shipment defined and met?

☐ Is verification of compliance documented and retained?

4.5 Document Control

☐ Are elements of the transfer documents forwarded to the appropriate parties?

☐ Do you readily remove obsolete documents from the areas?

4.8 Product Identification and Traceability

☐ Are procedures in place to ensure traceability?

☐ Are your products marked per your requirements?

4.12 Inspection and Test Status

☐ Do you maintain procedures for the verification of requirements, and are the verification records easily available?

4.15 Handling, Storage, Packaging, and Delivery

☐ Have you developed a comprehensive set of procedures addressing handling, storage, packaging, postinspection, and test handling and delivery availability?

4.16 Quality Records

☐ Do your procedures identify the proper handling, sorting, and storage of shipping records?

☐ Are these records easily retrieved and are they accurate?

4.18 Training

☐ Are employee training records reviewed regularly to ensure adequacy and conformance?

☐ Are employees who are involved in the physical movement of materials fully qualified with supporting training documents?

Servicing

4.1 Management Responsibility

☐ Are your quality policy and objectives documented?

☐ Is your organization trained and does it understand your quality policy?

☐ Are there job descriptions that define authority and responsibility for servicing?

☐ Is there a formal organization established for in-house auditing that is adequately staffed and trained?

4.3 Contract Review

☐ Are there procedures established to support customer inquiries?

☐ Are the requirements for service contracts defined?

☐ Are order preparation and review procedures established to ensure customers' requests can be satisfied?

☐ Are methods established for clarification of orders with customers?

☐ Are there verification procedures to ensure proper translation of customer orders into internal work orders?

☐ Are communications to customers formalized?

4.5 Document Control

☐ Are your service procedures reviewed and authorized by the appropriate personnel?

☐ Do you have documentation control procedures that ensure the availability of current documents at the appropriate locations and the removal of obsolete documents?

☐ Are changes to documents approved by an authorized individual and identified through a revision document?

4.8 Product Identification and Traceability
☐ Do you have formal methods and procedures for the anticipation and identification of needed spare parts?

4.9 Process Control
☐ Do you have procedures that clearly identify methods for the establishment of servicing schedules and results?
☐ Have you identified any special processes and qualified the individuals to perform the task and inspections?
☐ Are the correct work instructions and equipment available for those performing the tasks?

4.10 Inspection and Testing
☐ Do you have inspection and test procedures for all the products you service?

4.11 Inspection, Measuring, and Test Equipment
☐ Do the inspection and test criteria include the equipment and software to be used, and are they appropriate for the task defined?
☐ When performing inspection, are the appropriate materials and equipment available, and are they maintained to the correct precision as defined by your calibration program?
☐ Does the test equipment have an indicator of the current calibration status?
☐ Are these tools and indicators safeguarded from unauthorized adjustments?
☐ Do you perform a reinspection when your testing equipment is found to be out of calibration or malfunctioning?
☐ Can you produce records to prove the reinspection?
☐ Are methods established for the proper care and storage of the test equipment and software?

☐ Are regular checks performed on the test equipment and software to verify conformance?

4.12 Inspection and Test Status

☐ Do inspection procedures require the identification of test status by marking, location, or supporting documents?

☐ Is there a formally designated individual or group responsible for determination and action related to nonconforming products or materials?

4.13 Control of Nonconforming Product

☐ Are there procedures for the handling and disposition of nonconforming products?

☐ Do these procedures include responsibility for review and authorization for release?

☐ Do nonconforming products that require corrective action remain identified as nonconforming until inspection is complete?

☐ Are nonconforming products separated and remain identified as nonconforming until final disposition?

4.15 Handling, Storage, Packaging, and Delivery

☐ Have you developed a comprehensive set of procedures addressing handling, storage, packaging, postinspection, and test handling and delivery availability?

4.16 Quality Records

☐ Do your records include repair activities, customer complaints, test equipment calibration records, products you support, and the cause of a breakdown for corrective action?

4.18 Training

☐ Are training records of service employees reviewed regularly to ensure adequacy and conformance?

❏ Can you ensure that employees trained on only specific equipment work on only that equipment?

4.19 Servicing

❏ Do your procedures require verification that your actions met the specified requirements?

Appendix 2

For More Information

Quality Improvement Programs and ISO 9000 Training
Qualtec Quality Services, Inc.
Phone: 407-775-8300   Fax: 407-775-8301
Contact: Bob Ricker

ISO 9000 News and Directory of Registered Companies
Quality Systems Update
Phone: 703-250-5900   Fax: 703-250-5313

Foxboro's ISO 9000 Registrar
Det Norske Veritas
Phone: 713-579-9003   Fax: 713-579-1360

For Official Copies of the ISO 9000 Standard
ASQC
Phone: 414-272-8575   Fax: 414-272-1734

To Reach The Authors
John T. Rabbitt   Peter A. Bergh
The Foxboro Company   The Foxboro Company
M.S. N05-3A   M.S. B51-1D
33 Commercial St.   33 Commercial St.
Foxboro, MA 02035   Foxboro, MA 02035

Phone: 508-549-2985   Phone: 508-549-2570
     or 508-582-4922
Fax: 508-549-4639   Fax: 508-549-4469

Index